G000162595

Disclaimer

The information included in this book is designed to provide helpful information on the subjects discussed. This book is not meant to be used to diagnose or treat any medical condition. For diagnosis or treatment of any medical problem, consult your own doctor. The author and publisher are not responsible for any specific health or allergy needs that may require medical supervision and are not liable for any damages or negative consequences from any application, action, treatment or preparation, to anyone reading or following the information in this book. Links may change and any references included are provided for informational purposes only.

Herbs and Spices

The Top 100 Best Herbs and Spices from Around the World

By Susan Hollister

Copyright © 2019

Table of Contents

CHAPTER 3: DEFINITION/DIMENSION HERBS AND SPICES 66

CHAPTER 4: EXOTIC HERBS AND SPICES .. 91

CHAPTER 5: DELIGHTFUL CITRUS FLAVORED HERBS AND SPICES 120

CHAPTER 6: HOT AND FIERY HERBS AND SPICES 140

CHAPTER 7: SWEET AND SPICY HERBS AND SPICES 159

Introduction

Congratulations, you have made a great decision in purchasing this book filled with the best herbs and spices from around the world! Get excited, because you are about to discover some your new favorite taste sensations! In the following pages you will learn about a wide variety of spices and herbs that you may have never heard of, along with their history, health benefits, how to grow them yourself and the best ways to incorporate them into your daily meals in new, fun and exciting ways!

I believe herbs and spices to be miracles, because they not only flavor your food, but they can also heal and have a wide variety of incredible benefits depending on which herb or spice you are using. The monks in the Middle Ages grew extensive herb gardens and the Chinese have been using herbs and spices as remedies for thousands of years. It's always nice when you can enjoy delicious and flavorful meals while helping yourself to heal all naturally.

Most herbs and spices have benefits, such as helping you to digest better, strengthening your body, reducing inflammation, relief from stomach cramps, along with helping with insomnia, anxiety and depression.

The 100 herbs and spices in this book are separated into chapters by their flavor profile. These categories include: Mediterranean, Earthy, Dimension and Definition, Exotic, Citrus, Hot and Fiery and Sweet and Spicy. You can use these herbs and spices in foods to gain their benefits or drink them as a tea.

If you would like completed recipes for each of the herbs and spices listed in this book, then be sure to check out my companion book to this one titled: Cooking with Spices and Herbs: 100 Savory Cookbook Recipes Featuring the Best Spices and Herbs from Around the World by Susan Hollister.

Get ready, because you are about to discover some of your new favorite herbs and spices that will fill your life with new and incredible taste sensations that you have never experienced before!

Chapter 1: Mediterranean Herbs and Spices

Mediterranean herbs and spices are those that originally grew in the Mediterranean region, particularly Rome/Italy and in Greece. Fortunately, most of the Mediterranean herbs are relatively simple to grow in the backyard garden and dry by hanging in a dark, dry area. These herbs have been in use for cooking, in remedies and symbolic gestures for ages. They originally grew near the sea in dry conditions. Mediterranean herbs are very drought tolerant and grow in the ground as easily as they grow in containers. The following herbs have their origin in the Mediterranean and work well with Italian and Greek food but should not be limited to those cuisines only. They are good with many different foods.

Basil

Basil's formal name is Ocimum basilicum and is from the mint family. There are many varieties including ornamental purple basil to elephant basil with large leaves. My favorite is Genovese because I feel it has the best flavor for cooking and it is potent for remedies. Globe basil has tiny leaves that form a globe-like bush and also are good for cooking.

Leaves are bright green and the stems are square and woody, like mint stems. They stand upright and bush out a bit reaching up to 12 inches high. The flowers grow on stalks or umbels and are usually white. I pinch of the flowers before they bloom because this signals the time for growing is almost over and I want my basil to keep growing all summer.

The flavor of basil is almost peppery, like a mild anise with some mint mixed in. It is very aromatic. The leaves are used dried, frozen or fresh. If you dry your own, it is possible to air dry leaves but they will turn dark and almost black. That does not change the flavor though. If you want green leaves, dry between paper towels in the microwave at 1 minute intervals until dry. Store dried basil in an airtight container out of the light and away from heat. Freezing the leaves does make the leaves a little slimy and dark, but if you are just tossing them in sauce, soups or stews it won't matter. Chop fresh leaves to use in recipes immediately.

Growing it in the garden is easy it is advisable to grow basil with tomatoes and peppers because it safeguards against harmful insects and also makes the tomatoes and peppers taste better. Basil is also great for growing in a pot. Basil needs full sun and even moisture and it will grow like crazy. Pinch the flower stalks off and use at will.

Basil is one of the Mediterranean Herbs that are very drought tolerant and grow in just about any soil. It is most commonly used in Greek and Italian cooking and the Egyptians used it for embalming their mummies.

Use basil in the kitchen with tomatoes. A famous salad is sliced tomatoes, sliced mozzarella cheese and a sprinkling of basil leaves with some oil and vinegar. I like basil in a grilled cheese sandwich with mozzarella and a thin sliced tomato slice. Basil goes great with garlic, olives, oregano, hummus and is an ingredient in pesto sauce. Make your own by combining 2 cups basil leaves, 2 cloves peeled garlic, ½ teaspoon lemon juice, ¼ teaspoon Kosher salt, 2 grinds of black pepper and ½ cup grated Parmesan cheese in a food processor. Process while adding ½ cup olive oil until it makes a nice paste. Add 2 to 3 tablespoons pine nuts and you are ready to use with pasta, on chicken or with beef.

Health benefits about with basil. It is especially helpful to guard against stomach upset from spicy foods so use it liberally with tomato sauce or with peppers. Make tea by steeping leaves fresh or dry in boiled water and drink for nausea and gas. A substance in basil relaxes blood vessels making it good for cardiovascular issues and blood flow. Basil is also an anti-inflammatory. Basil has antibacterial properties and was used as an antibiotic in Rome and Greece.

Add near the end of cooking to retain the flavor. Freeze in ice cube trays with a little water, pop the cubes out and save in a recloseable bags in the freezer and just pop a few in a soup or stew recipe. You can even wash down the kitchen cupboards with tea to clean and get rid of germs.

Bay

Other names for this delicious leaf are sweet bay, Oregon myrtle, California laurel, Poet's laurel, Roman laurel or bay laurel.

Bay leaves are grown on a large shrub that sometimes can grow up to a monstrous 60 feet. The leaves are long and lance shaped and a lovely gray green color. It is common to dry the leaves for use in cooking and the leaves are added whole and removed before serving. The leaves are quite tough and leathery. The shrub also produces berries, but they are not used in cooking. The leaves can be used dried, fresh or frozen. The most pungent manner is to use them dried. Bay leaves need special conditions to grow, so it is just better to purchase them as they are inexpensive.

The ancient Romans used bay as a symbol of honor. Wreaths adorned both Roman and Greek scholars and heroes. The herb was originally used medicinally, but the flavor lends well to cooking having a sharp and stringent taste. It has a bitter flavor with a touch of floral and gives food a savory punch. I know when I forget to put the bay leaf in my stew, there is something missing.

Bay is often used in soups, stews and sauces and is usually best used with slow cooked dishes like pasta sauce, beef stew and chicken noodle soup. Bay is included in the combination called "Bouquet Garni" used with all types of meat, fish and in pickling. I prefer to use dried leaves, but if you are in an area where the temperature is moderate and can get fresh leaves. Never break up a bay leave always keeping it whole and always remove it before eating the dish. The bay leaf can cause serious problems if eaten. The texture is hard to break down and can get stuck in the digestive system causing a bowel blockage or it can get stuck in the esophagus and cause choking.

Bay leaves can be frozen and last about 2 to 3 years while dried leaves last about six months if kept in an airtight container in a dark, cool place. Turkish grown bay is much stronger in flavor than the California type but it is also more expensive.

Bay has traditionally been used to benefit the digestive system. The herb eases gas and enhance bile flow. Bay is said to produce insulin making it lower blood sugar and it also is said to lower cholesterol. Bay has a compound called eugenol, which is an anti-inflammatory, anti-fungal and antioxidant. It is also said to help migraines. The best way to utilize bay for these things is to make a tea by steeping a few leaves in a couple cups of boiling water in a teapot. Avoid this tea and excess use of bay if pregnant because it was once used to aid in abortions. Another good use for bay is to make a paste and apply to areas where arthritis is a problem.

Garlic

You either love garlic or you don't and garlic is one of the most used herbs out there. It is used in all types of cuisines, not just one or two and garlic is known and used the world over. Garlic is in the same family as onions, chives, shallots and leeks. The parts used is the bulb that grows under ground as opposed to the tubular snake-like green leaves that grow about 3 feet above ground. The bulb has different sections that are called cloves and they are covered in a layer of dry, papery skin that is removed. Each bulb has 10 to 20 cloves and is best used fresh. Garlic comes in other forms besides fresh. It comes chopped in oil, dried into powder, combined with salt to make garlic salt and it is also easily used frozen.

Garlic has a strong flavor all its own and it can be strong or mellow. The strongest flavor is eating garlic raw and the more you cook it or expose it to heat, it mellows. Therefore, if you want a strong garlic flavor in a dish, don't cook it long. The most mellow flavor occurs when the whole bulb is roasted. The garlic gets very soft inside the cloves and when you squirt it out, it is simply delicious and very mellow.

The ancient Greeks and Romans were garlic lovers. They originally used the herb for medicine and it still can be used that way today. It is the oldest cultivated crop of record. Garlic has a mysterious side too. It was given to the pyramid builders to give them strength and endurance, it was offered to the gods and fed to athletes and warriors. During the middle ages, it was thought to protect against the evil eye and, of course, it keeps pesky vampires away. In Egypt it was even used as a form of currency.

Too bad we can't use it like money today because it is very easy to grow. Just take a clove with all the paper on it and plant it pointed end up about 3 to 5 inches down in soft ground. I live in a moderate climate where we do have snow in the winter and I plant my cloves near the end of the fall. They come up in the spring after it gets warm. Once the stems growing above ground start turning yellowish brown, I knock them down breaking the stalks and then dig up the bulbs once the stalks turn brown and crispy. Let the bulbs dry on newspaper a few days out of bright sunlight to cure them. Mine go in the garage and then I braid the stalks and hang stalks with bulbs attached in my basement and use at will.

Garlic works well in savory dishes including soups and stews. Spaghetti sauce would not be the right without it. Rub a clove inside a wooden salad bowl and make salad in it. Put a little raw, minced garlic in salad dressings too. Garlic goes well with just about any meat, chicken or fish and with most vegetables. Mince it, chop it, squish it through a garlic press or use whole cloves in recipes or opt for garlic powder. To roast garlic, drizzle with olive oil, wrap a bulb in foil and roast in a pan at 400 degrees F for 1 hour. Let it cool a bit and unwrap. The cloves will fall apart and squeeze gooey, amazing paste from the cloves.

Garlic is thought to boost the immune system just by eating it. Some people eat cloves raw to control blood pressure and cholesterol. It is said to help the common cold and a nasty cough. It is even said to improve the memory. Garlic does make your breathe smell and your hands if you touch it. Use mouthwash or toothpaste to neutralize the smell or take a silver spoon and rub it on your hands to get rid of the sulfur smell.

Greek Oregano

Greek Oregano is one of the three main oreganos (Greek, Italian and Mexican) and is probably the spicier and more flavorful. Another name for Greek oregano is rigani and the plant grows about 4 feet tall with little white flowers. The leaves are oval, dark green in color, fuzzy and about 5/8 inches long. They turn light when the leaves are dry. Greek oregano tends to be a little bushier than the other types. Leaves are most often used for cooking, but the flowers can be thrown in a salad too. Use fresh, dried or frozen leaves in dishes to make them deliciously hot and spicy.

Greek oregano, of course, originated in Greece and was and still is used for erosion control along the coast. Traditionally it was used as wreaths to encircle the heads of brides and grooms at Greek weddings and placed on tombs of the dead to give them peace.

Greek oregano may have originated in Greece, but you can grow it just about anywhere. All it needs is full sun and well drained soil. In Greece it has only rocky soil and sea water, so growing in your garden should be very successful. The plant does not like large quantities of rain and prefers to dry out between watering and in cold climates two to three harvests cut 3 inches above the ground should be possible before winter sets in. Greek oregano likes warmer weather and should be treated as an annual in cold climates. However, it is easily grown in a pot and can be brought in during the winter. It just needs a great deal of light and window light probably won't keep it going all winter. Try to pick off the flowers when they appear to keep it growing.

Greek oregano adds flavor to tomato sauce, fish, eggs, chicken, beef, lamb and pork. Sprinkle some into cheese and eggs and add to salads. Greek oregano gives a peppery flavor to vegetables. Try it with zucchini, green beans, carrots, cauliflower and other veggies. Chop tomatoes and add to them, scramble eggs with a little salt and pepper and serve the tomatoes on top of the cooked eggs. Add to grilled cheese or macaroni and cheese for a different flavor. A great marinade for meats and fish is to use ¼ cup lemon juice with a little salt and pepper and ½ cup olive oil adding about 2 teaspoons dried Greek oregano.

Greek oregano is a natural anti-inflammatory and anti-fungal. A little tea will help indigestion and soothe a dry cough. It is also known to bring on menstruation, so pregnant women should use it sparingly in cooking. Greek oregano has a high thymol content and works as an antiseptic. You can wash down your shower and it will get rid and prevent any mildew that might form. A little tea dabbed on eczema might help and hot tea will get rid of gas.

Fennel

Fennel has another name of sweet anise and it does taste similar to anise; however, it is rarely used in making any sweet dish. Fennel adds a bit of fresh spicy flavor to savory dishes as a hint of anise or licorice.

Romans wrote of the medicinal achievements of this herb long before they started eating it for pleasure. It has been utilized by healers as a medicinal herb all through the ages and travelled far and wide. During the Middle Ages fennel was thought to keep away evil spirits and King Edward I of England used it on his table as a condiment. The puritans brought it with them to the United States not to dispel evil or to eat for pleasure, but because nibbling on it helped to keep their stomachs silent during their long and elaborate church services.

Fennel is a large bulb that grows underground and has feathery leaves that rise from the ground on stocks looking like dill. Fennel is crunchy, like an onion, and even looks like a pale green onion. Fennel cannot be cured or kept long out of the ground like an onion and must be used soon after it is pulled. The pretty leaves, or fronds, are can be used as garnish and can be eaten. The stalks are added to long cooked foods as they will soften. The bulb is often sliced, eaten raw or cooked and lends a sweet flavor to dishes.

Fennel is easily grown in a backyard garden and looks very pretty. It needs full sine and likes cooler weather. In warm climates it is planted in late winter and harvested in the spring while in cold climates, it is planted mid-summer and harvested just before the snow flies.

Fennel makes a delightful addition to salads, soups and sauces. One of the best salads I ever had was when fennel was sliced thin and added to fresh greens along with orange segments and red onion dressed Italian dressing. It goes very well with chicken and fish. My favorite way to serve is to put in a chicken stir fry or add to a pasta with white or basic olive oil sauce. It goes very well with Italian sausage and red sauce too. Serve it raw, sautéed, cooked or braised. Braise wedges of fennel with some tomatoes, olives and capers in a little water for a lovely vegetable dish. Par boil the fennel first so it softens. Take slices and coat them with egg and breadcrumbs. Put them in an airfryer or deep fry them. Par boil slices of fennel with potato slices, drain and layer with grated Parmesan and bake about 20 minutes with some butter on top. Sauté with just about any vegetable for a sweet and aromatic flavor.

If you take any type of beta blockers, watch your intake of fennel. Fennel is full of potassium, calcium, iron and zinc making it great for health of bones in the body. It is said to decrease blood pressure and increase immune system being an anti-inflammatory. A little fennel tea will help constipation or digestive issues.

Lavender

Lavender is a Mediterranean herb that most people don't think about using in culinary dishes. It is an integral part in the herbal blend Herbs de Provence and has been used with food for centuries as well as for scenting clothing and rooms or using in remedies.

Lavender has a very sweet scent and some people think it tastes too much like soap in cooking, but others love the floral flavor it imparts.   English lavender (Munstead) is probably the best lavender for cooking because it has less scent.   Some herb companies do sell what they call "culinary lavender" that is not so strong. Lavender has pretty blue green oval leaves that grow up the stem looking like spikes and the plant is ever green.   The flowers grow up a central spike and are light to dark purple. It is the flower that is used but leaves also have the flavor. It is used fresh or dried.

Growing lavender is very easy and the bush it grows on makes a great addition to any garden. Some lavender is very hardy and will come back year after year. I had a shrub that lasted 10 years and grew very large. The stems got extremely woody and it didn't produce many leaves or flowers at the end and had to be replaced, which made me very sad. It needs full sun to partial shade and will produce more flowers in sun. Clip off the flowers that grow on long thin stalks before they open, if possible, and bunch with a rubber band hanging them upside down to dry in a warm, dry area out of the sun. Keep in airtight containers after that. If using fresh, just clip the stems and put them in a glass of water in the refrigerator for about 1 week.

There is documentation of lavender being used medicinally during the Roman era. Romans used it in their famous baths and it was brought to France where it is grown in beautiful fields of purple. It went from France to Spain, Italy and England. The English cultivated it to new levels as Queen Elizabeth I loved the scent. They brought it to America.

Watch how much lavender you use in cooking because it can make food taste soapy. Just the right amount will make a savory dish you will never forget. Lavender goes great with any grilled meat. In most cases, ½ teaspoon dried or 1 teaspoon fresh will season it adequately. I love it on beef or lamb, but it is also great with chicken. Lavender is used in salads where the purple stands out against the greens. A little lavender sprinkled on sliced strawberries, blue berries or peaches with a little honey and lemon or orange juice makes a great summer dessert. Lavender is often used in baked goods like cakes, bread and cookies and I love lavender sorbet.

Lavender has long been used cosmetically and the Romans noticed early on it healed and softened skin as well as scented the body beautifully. It is antiseptic and heals burns including sunburn. I keep a vial of lavender oil in my kitchen and rub it on burns which rarely blister and might even be healed by morning. The tea actually tastes great, but this is one tea I actually suggest sweetening with a little honey or the lavender is a little overwhelming. Tea is said to stop vomiting, gas, intestinal cramps, indigestion, headache and some symptoms of PMS. Rubbing oil on a sore tooth is reported to stop pain for just a little while.

Marjoram

Marjoram has another name of sweet marjoram because it does have a sweetish flavor. It is in the mint family and like oregano with marjoram being milder. It is a perennial and the plant is low growing rarely getting more than 12-inches high with square stems and small oval green leaves. The leaves are used in cooking and can be dry, fresh or frozen preferable in an ice cube tray with water. The flavor is slightly camphor-like with a warm and slightly sweet taste.

The herb was used to make wreaths worn at weddings because it was in association with the goddess of love, Aphrodite had a love. It is very easy to grow in the garden or in containers and because it is low growing, it is perfect for an edging or at the edge of a pot to cascade down. The flowers attract butterflies and bees. Marjoram needs to be in full sun and isn't picky about soil. In the Mediterranean region, it grows in dry rocky soil so any soil will do. Remove flowers to encourage more leaf growth and harvest, bundling sprigs with a rubber band and hanging to dry in a dry area out of the sun. Dried leaves should be stored in airtight containers.

Marjoram goes well with many things and is an herb no kitchen should be without. It goes with any meat or vegetable and is good to enhance salad dressing or egg dishes. Goat cheese with a little marjoram mixed in is delightful and I love it in an egg and potato frittata. It pares well with garlic and parsley. Throw a little on beef, chicken, lamb and pork or opt to sprinkle it over cauliflower, corn, mushrooms, eggplant, summer squash or zucchini and add some to cooked carrots with a bit of lemon juice. It goes nicely with marinades, soups and stews and gives tomatoes, tomato sauce and salsa a nice extra flavor.

Marjoram is good for digestion so if you are eating spicy food that might disagree with you, make a little marjoram tea to settle things down. It has enzymes that break food down better and relieve gas, constipation and stomach cramps. It is antifungal and antibacterial and is said to prevent colds and flu. It is even said to ease the pain of food poisoning. Marjoram is said to also help with high blood pressure, high cholesterol and migraines. It is a therapy herb helping with mood and anxiety.

Oregano

In the Mediterranean region, oregano was called "Joy of the Mountain" because it grew on the sides of the mountains. Ancient Greeks believed cattle that ate the oregano had the most delicious meat and this is an herb that originated in Greece. Romans also enjoyed the flavor and on their military campaigns, they brought it to other regions through Europe and as far as North Africa. People of the Middle Ages used oregano as a medication and it was considered good luck and good health if you grew it in your garden. Soldiers during World War II brought the herb to the United States and it has been a popular one ever since.

Other names for oregano include wild marjoram, Spanish thyme and European oregano. It too, is in the mint family and sports square stems and small fuzzy oval green leaves with small purple flowers. The plant stems are shrub-like and woody and certain types grow upright or creep along the ground.   The plant grows well in both the ground and in containers and needs full sun and well drained, slightly dry soil. Always pinch of the flowers to make the plant bushier and producing leaves.   The flavor is like marjoram but stronger. Leaves are used either fresh, frozen or dried for cooking.

Oregano is used mostly in Greek and Italian cuisine and is especially desired when cooking with tomatoes. It is also great with most vegetables and meats. Use it in soups, salads, in chili or in marinades. It works well with chicken, beans, eggs, cheeses and fish.

The Greeks believed oregano was an antidote to poison and does tend to soothe digestive problems like upset stomach, diarrhea and nausea. It is antibacterial and anti-inflammatory and used in a paste; it can ease the pain of muscle pain and arthritis. Dab a little tea on cold sores, aches and pains, on the head for headaches and wash hair in the tea to get rid of dandruff. It might even help problems with a sore throat or acne.

Parsley

I think everyone has had an encounter with parsley, either in a dish or garnishing a dish. Parsley has a mild yet bitter flavor and it is a bit bland, but you know when it isn't there and it should be. It tends to brighten the flavor of food.

There are two types of parsley. The flatleaf, Italian type is the kind most used for flavor and has flat lobed leaves that are spring green. The curly type has curly leaves and looks very full and green and it is used mostly for garnish because it does not have good flavor. Both types have hollow stems and many branched leaves and the flowers are tiny and bright yellow. Never let your parsley flower because it will be very bitter. The plants grow about 12 inches but can reach up to 40 inches. The leaves are what is used in cooking and are used fresh, frozen or dried.

Parsley first started to grow on Greek hillsides and, at first, were used as a symbol of death. Legend tells that wherever the blood of Archemorus dripped on the ground, there would grow parsley. Romans used parsley to freshen their breath and it does actually do that. They would hide the fact that they were drinking wine by chewing parsley and yes, that does work and I did it when a teen. During the Jewish holiday of Passover, parsley is used on the Seder plate to symbolize rebirth.

Parsley takes an extraordinary long amount of time to grow from seed and it is not suggested to start in pots and replant because it does not like to be moved either. Legend says that germination takes so long because it travels three times to the devil before it breaks through the ground. I live in a cold climate and plant my seeds in the ground a few weeks before the last frost and keep the area protected. The seeds sprout anywhere from 5 to 6 weeks later, sometimes even longer. I have tried to buy transplants and have been able to grow them in pots but they look like they are going to wilt and die long before they perk up. Just keep them watered, but not waterlogged, and they will start to grow. Plant in full sun and well-drained soil. Parsley will also take partial shade. It is a biennial, so the first year you will get a harvest and the second year it comes up only to set seed. Make sure you let some of it seed because you will have parsley popping up in the spring and have a bumper crop. I dry my own parsley by placing it on a fine screen and let it sit in a dark dry place until the leaves dry. Dried parsley will last about 6 months in an airtight container and fresh will last a few days in a glass of water in the refrigerator. Frozen parsley comes out limp and I only use it in soups and stews.

Parsley is great in salads or in sauces and marinades. It goes well with eggs including frittatas or with cheese in quiche. Use with beef, chicken, lamb, fish and pork. It is especially good with lentils and beans or hummus. Sprinkle over mashed, baked or boiled potatoes or opt for a little on salted French fries. Parsley enhances the flavor of tomatoes, green beans, zucchini, squash and other vegetables. In the Mideast they use a great deal of parsley in their couscous, tabbouleh salad and with their meats. Parsley pretty much goes with anything and makes a great garnish too.

Healthwise, parsley is very useful. It is endowed with a large amount of Vitamin C and has been used to treat rickets. It boosts the immune system and fights allergies and is an anti-inflammatory. It reduces pain and swelling of arthritis when using the oil because it has pain killing eugenol. Folic acid in parsley keeps blood vessels clear and flowing and also works as a diuretic. Use in smoothies to help with detox and general health. Be careful if you take blood thinners because it can prevent clotting of the blood. It also contains Vitamin K that promote bone health.

Rosemary

Rosemary symbolizes remembrance in the language of flowers and often show up in wedding bouquets or wreaths for tombstones of the dead. Other names are "Dew of the Sea" and "Rose of Mary". Legend has it that the flowers of rosemary used to be white, but Mary, mother of Jesus, spread her cloak over a rosemary bush and the flowers turned blue, like her cloak, to honor her.

Rosemary is an evergreen shrub grown originally in the Mediterranean region. The leaves are needle-like and green with small purple to blue flowers. The shrubs are woody and many branched. The flavor is somewhat pine-like but it doesn't taste like you are eating a Christmas tree. The flavor is fresh, bitter and astringent. Grow rosemary in your garden or in a container. I suggest getting a transplant. In warm regions it will grow very big and bushy, but in cold regions it is hard to keep rosemary alive through the winter. The plant can take some cold temperatures and I once got mine to winter over in the breezeway between my house and garage by spritzing it with water occasionally. That was only once though. Rosemary needs full sun and good drainage. It is drought resistant so only water when the soil is dried out. Hang stems in bundles to dry out of the sun and then just run your fingers up the stem to remove the dried leaves. Store them in an airtight container or fresh in the refrigerator a few days. I've never had good luck with frozen rosemary.

Rosemary was originally used by Greeks and Romans as a medicinal herb. It was grown in monasteries during the Middle ages to help in healing. It was woven into wreaths for Greeks to make them smart as it was supposed to enhance memory and brain functions.

Rosemary pares well with garlic and is included in the herb blend of Bouquet Garni. It goes well with lamb, beef, chicken, and fish and enhances these meats by sprinkling it on or using in a marinade. Red potatoes with a teaspoon or more of butter and rosemary is very good and the herb goes great with fresh cooked peas, sautéed zucchini with squash and tomatoes. Crush the herb to get more flavor out of it. Put it in soups, stews, stuffing and even in fruit salads.

Rosemary is antibiotic and the oil has been used for ages to heal skin irritations, wounds and arthritis. Rub some tea into the head to get rid of dandruff and it is also said to darken graying hair. Rosemary tea helps the immune system work better, blood circulation, and may improve recovery from a stroke. The aroma is said to improve concentration. I always kept a little bottle of oil around when I was studying for tests during college. Sometimes it worked and sometimes it didn't.

Sage

Sage is one of my favorite herbs mostly because I love the bitter/sweet flavor with a little eucalyptus and citrus thrown in. It just tastes like home. It is a strong flavor, but one that I grew up with. My mother used to grow sage in the back yard and used it in bread stuffing for turkey and pork chops.

Sage is easily grown in the garden or in containers. If planted in the ground, it gets bigger and woodier every year. The leaves can be more than 1-inch long and they are a delightful light gray green, the same as the walls in my living room with a paint called "sage". The plant reaches about 2 feet tall in the ground and it is very bushy with purple, pink or white flowers growing at the top of the plant. It is best to remove the flowers when the bloom so that more leaves growing, but I do let some bloom and put them in salads. The leaves are best fresh, and I prefer dried over frozen.

The ancient Greeks and Romans used sage as a snake bit antidote. They used infused oil to invigorate the body and mind. Sage was a remedy for colds, fevers, and epilepsy during the Middle Ages. It was a cash crop being traded to China as a valuable herb.

Grow sage in the garden to get rid of insects that would normally harm other plants. It repels carrot fly and cabbage worm and mice hate it, so plant it around the base of your house to keep them out. Set transplants about 1 to 2 feet apart and mulch over in the winter with pine boughs so they will come back the next spring.

Originally sage was used medicinally just like most of the other Mediterranean herbs but it is very tasty and goes with many different foods. Use in loaf bread recipes and in bread stuffing. It is good in most sauces and in salads raw. Meats that are complimented by sage include poultry, pork, trout, lamb, sausage, and beef. It goes very well with eggs, polenta and risotto as well. Try sprinkling a little on just about any vegetable including tomatoes, beans, squash, carrots, cabbage, cauliflower and more.

Sage is an antiseptic and the tea kills bacteria on your countertops just as well as in your throat when you have a sore throat. It is said to kill the substance that causes cavities in the teeth. Sage is reported to help with hot flashes and aging skin. Eat the leaves, drink tea or dab some tea on your face to keep youthful appearances. Sage has over 160 polyphenols (chemical compounds) that are antioxidant and are said to reduce cholesterol, lower blood sugar, stop diarrhea and helps depression.

Thyme

Garden thyme, also called common thyme, is a relative to oregano and has the same tiny, delicious leaves. It grows very low to the ground or can cascade over the edge of a pot placed in a sunny spot in well-drained soil. Just like all Mediterranean herbs, let it dry out before watering and the herb was first used as medicine. Romans used the herb as a protective herb to protect homes and livelihood. It was associated with strength and sign of respect. Greeks burned it in their homes to give courage to the ones that lived or visited there. It was used during the black plague to cure or prevent the plague

The plant only grows to 6 or 12 inches high on woody stems with small oval leaves that are a pretty gray green. The flowers are white, pink and lilac and the leaves can be dried, frozen or used fresh. Dry thyme by hanging clumps in a dark warm place and strip the leaves off by running fingers down the stem.

Flavor bursts from the tiny leaves because of the compound of thymol that it has a delightfully strong flavor of pine with mint and registers as a cool flavor on the tongue. It goes with just about any grilled or roasted meat or seafood and works well with pasta and sauce, tomatoes, potatoes, zucchini, squash, broccoli, cauliflower, beans and more. When adding to food, crush dried thyme to release the oils before cooking and add early to get the oils going. Thyme works particularly well with long cooked dishes. It also compliments eggs and cheese and is often used in soups and stews. It is a part of both her blends of Bouquet Garni and Herbs de Province.

The thymol in the herb is particularly useful in many ways. I put a little thyme tea in my bath to stimulate the skin and to ease sunburn. It goes well with meat because it helps the body digest fatty foods better and it is said to lower cholesterol and blood pressure along with improving the immune system and moodiness. It is also a good tea to drink when having a cold, stuffy nose and sore throat. Thyme is an antibiotic and soldiers in World War I used it on wounds as a disinfectant in the field.

The next chapter presents earthy essential herbs and spices and
    are used with both
sweet and savory dishes.

Chapter 2: : Earthy Essential Herbs and Spices

Earthy flavors can be mild or strong. They can remind you of organic substances (and I do mean soil) or things that grow in soil like grasses, hay or things that grow in the garden. Onions are a great earthy flavor that is strong while poppyseed is something that is much milder, yet a very "from the earth" flavor. Earthy flavors enhance the food we eat.

Borage

Borage is an odd plant with big toothed hairy leaves that look a bit scraggly but have the most beautiful periwinkle blue flowers. It grows about 1 ½ foot high with hollow squarish stems that are hairy, white and prickly as are the wrinkled leaves. The flowers are big, starshaped and fall forward in clusters. Almost the entire plant is edible including stems, leaves and flowers if you can stand the hairy parts, but they do soften somewhat when cooking with them. The flavor is a wonderful fresh cucumber flavor in the leaves and stems. The flowers do not have much flavor but look pretty in dishes. My favorite way to fix borage is to boil the leaves and stems and eat like spinach.

Borage is known by several other name including star flower, bee plant and bee bread probably because bees flock to it for its nectar. Plant plants far apart in your garden or in containers because this plant spreads. If the plants get too close together, they tend to get mildew because air cannot flow through leaves that are too close.

Sauté leaves, stems and flowers in a little olive oil or butter with some chopped garlic and a few red pepper flakes for a nice side dish. Always wash the borage stems at least 2 times before cooking because those prickly hairs grab on to dirt and grime and hold on tight. Preserve the flowers in sugar and use on confectionaries or throw them in a salad for color. I use fresh leaves like lettuce in sandwiches and yes, the hairs do tickle a little as they go down, but the cucumber flavor is simply wonderful. My favorite sandwich is a combination of full or chopped leaves and flowers combined with a little cream cheese and yogurt.

I like to make tea with borage leaves and stems by steeping it in boiling water for about 15 minutes, covered. Add a little honey and the flavor is interesting and like cucumber. Not only is the tea good but it also is a great anti-inflammatory. This tea will get rid of a fever quick and ease the throat when infected with a cough. It also lifts your spirits a bit. It is good for bronchitis, PMS and does help regulate blood sugar. Steep leaves and stems in a little olive oil, strain and use it on your skin for inflammations or eczema.

Borage is best used fresh but you can freeze leaves and flowers in ice cube trays with water to throw in soups and stews or tea. I have dried the leaves but they just don't taste the same.

Those that have problems with their liver should eat borage in moderation.

Chamomile

Chamomile is also known as pot marigold, Scotch marigold, Mary-Gold, Mary-Bud and Poor Man's Saffron. It is a beautiful little daisy-like flower with a yellow to orange center on bright green feathery leaves. The two types of chamomile are Roman and German chamomile. The Roman type grows near the ground and is often used as ground cover, while the German type grows about 1 to 2 feet high and waves in the wind. The parts used are the flowers and they have a slight apple flavor with floral tones. The flowers also smell much like apples. When dried, the herb looks a little orange or yellow, which is how it got one of its nicknames of poor man's saffron. Dry the flower heads in a basket or in a brown paper bag sealed, both hung from the rafters so that air circulates all around to dry the flowers. Any little bit of moisture can cause mildew. I store my dried chamomile in canning jars in a cupboard so the light does not hit it directly. I love making chamomile tea and sweetening it with honey. It is a wonderful sleep and relaxation aid.

Chamomile was grown all over Europe and used originally for medication in ancient Rome, Greece and Egypt and then in the medieval monasteries in England and Europe. It is one of the nine sacred herbs written of in the Lacnunga Anglo Manuscript from the 1st millennium.

Chamomile is easy to grow. I had a whole bunch of Roman that grew on a rocky slope in my yard at one time. I didn't have to mow the slope and the flowers were very cheerful and attracted bees. German chamomile grows well in a garden or in containers and doesn't need anything special. It will grow in the most disgusting soil and literally grows like a weed. The flowers self-seed if you don't pick them off and I usually leave a few flowers on the plant at the end of the season to do just this.

Chamomile makes a relaxing and tasty tea and it is often used in desserts, with and other seafood, infused in liquor for cocktails, in lattes, with strawberries and cream, in strawberry or peach shortbread and in scones. I like putting it in smoothies and in sugar cookies. I have a friend that uses an infusion of chamomile to make her French macaroons.

If I cannot go to sleep, I make myself a cup of chamomile tea and I am down for the count. The tea will also helm an upset stomach, promote a strong immune system, may help the symptoms of a cold. I also use the tea on rough and inflamed skin issues. It may help with tension, including headaches and depression. It is an anti-inflammatory herb as well. Watch out if you are allergic to rag weed, because you might also be allergic to chamomile.

Chervil

Your best bet for buy chervil is in an upscale grocery store or just grow it in your garden. Chervil is also known as French Parsley and grows best in spring when temperatures are cool. The leaves look like flat leaf parsley. If you do grow it in the garden, do not let it flower because that makes the leaves very bitter. Pick them off. Chervil also wilts quickly so the stems need to stay moist and must be used soon after picking or bringing them home. The flavor of chervil is like parsley with tarragon and a little bit of mint and anise mixed in. It is a flavor all its own but it is a strong flavor. It fades with heat, so be sure to add it to cooked recipes at the end. Use the leaves and stems and discard the flowers.

Growing chervil is easy. Grow in the north in the spring and in the south in the winter. It tends to bolt and turn bitter in hot temperatures. Grow it in the ground or in containers. I like to put mine in window boxes and once it is done producing, I just plant flowers in the boxes. Do not put in full sun because it needs shade.

The origin of chervil is Europe and Asia on the Black and Caspian Sea. It is a favorite of French chefs. It is said that eating it makes your healthy and cheerful. Chervil is delicious in omelet or with eggs in general. It is in the mixture called fines herbes that is used in French cooking. Bearnaise and hollandaise sauce would be nothing without the flavor of chervil. Use with steak, fish or chicken or try it in a vinaigrette. It combines well with tarragon and parsley. Mix with soft butter, wrap in wax paper and store in the refrigerator. Top steamed vegetables and grilled meat with this incredible herbed butter and let it on top it. Use the butter in a frying pan and add some lemon zest and sliced zucchini for a lovely side dish. Chervil also goes great pounded into goat cheese or mixed in yogurt. Put it in potato salad for a fresh treat.

Chervil is high in vitamins A and C, calcium, iron, manganese, potassium and zinc. Chew some leaves when you have a stomachache and it might go away. It also tends to get rid of excess fluid and helps with kidney stones. You can eat a good quantity because it is very mild. Making a tea will help you use it up and help you to lose unwanted fluid in your body, but it will not flush everything out.

Use fresh only and store in plastic bag in the refrigerator using it up as soon as possible. Chervil does not dry very well and does not retain flavor when dried.

Chia Seed

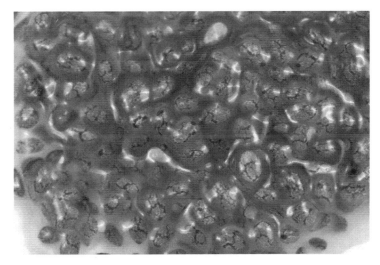

Chia seed is considered a superfood because of the many health benefits they provide. The only part of the chia plant that is consumed is the tiny black, white or gray seed that are only about 1 millimeter in diameter. They may be small when dry but when they are mixed with a liquid, they swell into a jelly-like mass. The seeds actually absorb up to 12 times their weight in liquid and look like fish eggs. Now that I've explained their very unappetizing appearance, I have to say the flavor is not bad. It is a mild nutty flavor with a little bit of a crunch. The whole seeds are soaked but in some recipes ground seed is also used.

You can't really grow chia seed in your back yard, but packages of them can be found almost anywhere. The plants were first cultivated by the Mayans and the Aztecs in Mexico and even then, they thought it to be a superfood and brought strength to those that ate them.

Chia seeds are gluten free and filled with fiber and omega 3 fatty acids. The are great sprinkled in a smoothie and give it a little bit of texture. They can also be sprinkled on backed goods just like poppy seed or sesame seed. Soaked chia seeds are a good substitute for eggs. About 1 tablespoon of dried seed in 3 tablespoons of water will equal one egg. Make sure to let the seed soak for about 5 minutes before using. Soaked seed also works as a binder in back goods or a thickener for sauces. Sprinkle in yogurt or cereal to give it a little crunch.

Chia is a great source of many essential nutrients including phosphorous, manganese, calcium, and potassium and they are low in calories. If you mix it in water (I use lemon water) they keep you from being hungry. I sip on some chia seed lemon water almost every morning to keep me from getting hungry before noon. The seeds introduce good bacteria to the intestines and help you to purge waste better. There is also some protein in the seed. They also strengthen bones, control blood sugar and help with any inflammation in the body. If you are going to use chia water, take it slow because you will be running to the bathroom often until you get used to it.

Cilantro

Cilantro is traditionally used with Latino style dishes but, apparently, the Chinese also appreciate this herb because it is also called Chinese parsley. It does look like parsley and comes from the same family but is a brighter green and the plant grows 8-inches to 1 foot high. Cilantro does double duty in the herb and spice world because the leaves are used to flavor and are called cilantro and the seeds are also harvested, dried and used in cooking but have a different flavor and different name of coriander. The flavor of cilantro is very fresh, but you must watch how much you use because it can become too strong and overpowering masking the flavor of the foods it is supposed to enhance.

Grow cilantro in your own garden. It gets nice a bushy and the leaves are used fresh only. If you try to dry it, it will taste like nothing. Plant early in the spring or late in fall because it does not like hot weather and will go to seed to quickly in warm temperatures. Interestingly enough, a bit of cilantro was found in an archeological dig in a cave in Israel that was dated back about 1000 years and it was thought to be used by the Egyptians. The

British brought the herb with them to America and it was one of the first cultivated North American crops.

Cilantro is not totally enjoyed by the Latino or Chinese community. It also appears in Italian, Indian and other Asian recipes. It does go exceedingly well with jalapeno peppers, however. Cilantro should not be cooked but served room temperature being sprinkled on top of the dish. The flavor will cook right out of it if you try. It goes well with chicken, fish and other seafood. Make a sauce using coconut milk, garlic, ginger and curry and then use cilantro to bring it some zing. Cilantro is found in salsa, gazpacho, chili and goes very well with cream sauces, eggs, and cheese. I use cilantro flavored herb butter to make chicken and eggs and it is very easy to make. Just soften some butter and put it on wax paper. Knead in chopped fresh cilantro so it is well combined and roll it into a log. Wrap in plastic wrap or leave it in the wax paper securing it on the ends tightly so it doesn't dry out. Keep it in the refrigerator and cut off a medallion to use. It will keep about a week or two in the refrigerator.

Not only is cilantro tasty, but it is good for you too. Cilantro gets rid of heavy metals in the body and helps the body cleanse itself from harmful toxins. Chemicals in cilantro help to keep the heart beating well and balances blood sugar. It has antioxidants that help the brain and alleviates anxiety with no nasty side effects as chemicals. It is also an anti-inflammatory and has enough vitamin A to be good for the eyes, skin and immune system.

Dill

There is more to dill than just pickles. It is a very versatile herb with a delicate, grassy flavor mixed with a little bit of spicy anise. Dill is native to West Africa, Russia and the Mediterranean and mention of it is found in Egyptian hieroglyphics, in Greek and Roman texts and even in medicinal writings by Hippocrates. Charlemagne always had it at his table because it would settle the stomachs of guests who ate too much.

Dill is a very tall plant, about 3 feet and it is very pretty. The delicate lacy fronds blow in the wind and the flowers grow resembling Queen Anne's Lace in clusters on an umbel, but they are a bright yellow. Flowers and leaves make for a beautiful garnish on foods and the seeds are used in many different cooking applications. I like to use fresh dill, but I also use dried fronds called dillweed. Plant in a sunny area with well drained soil. It grows best in cooler temperatures and I like to grow mine against a fence for protection against wind. I have seen it tied up with a large tomato cage and that seems to do the trick too. Harvest leaves any time and use or dry and let some of the flowers go to seed. When seed forms and starts to turn brown, cut the whole stem, bundle several together and put a brown paper lunch bag

43

over top securing with string or rubber bands. Hang in a dark, dry area. This way the seeds will fall into the bag rather than on the ground.

Dill is popular with cucumbers to make pickles or any other picked vegetable like peppers or tomatoes. It is often part of the recipe for cabbage dishes and cold soups. I like to put some in homemade ranch dressing. Add to melted butter and pour over a baked potato for a real treat. Dill brings plain old cottage cheese and yogurt to life and can be added to vegetable dip. Use it in egg dishes, egg salad and with salmon and other fish. It goes great with chicken and lamb or bake a loaf of dill bread. It enhances the flavor of peas, squash, beets asparagus, cauliflower and other vegetables.

Dill has been used in remedies for ages and is a great digestive aid. It calms the stomach, stops gas and heartburn. Colicky babies are often given gripe water, which is water with dill infused in it and it calms their stomach quickly. Dill water will also cure a case of hiccups too. It gets rid unwanted organisms in the stomach and replaces them with good bacteria in the digestive tract. 1 tablespoon of seed has as much calcium in it as 1/3 cup of milk. It clears congestion, is said to get rid of headaches and cleanses the breath. Just chew on the seeds and see what happens.

Store leaves fresh in the refrigerator about 2 weeks and freeze by chopping in a blender with a little water and pouring in ice cube trays. Once the cube forms, pop it out and put it in a freezer bag in the freezer. Dry seed and dillweed will stay fresh in an airtight container about 1 year.

Flax

Flaxseed is considered an herb because it does flavor food, but it also considered a health food. It has a beautiful nutty flavor that is very mild and gives food a little crunch. It was originally used as a fiber supplement, but then the flavor was discovered and it was used in culinary dishes. It was first cultivated in Egypt and now all over the world. The seed is the only part of the plant that is used. Seeds are ground to make meal or flower and used in baking. Flax flour needs to be refrigerated and has a short shelf life so only buy what you need and can use in a few days. The crushed seed is also used and that lasts longer.

The flax plant grows about 2 feet tall and it seems a waste that only the seed is used. Fortunately, the plant is also used to create woven cloth, which is two to three times stronger than cotton. The seed must be toasted or baked to eat because raw flaxseed contains toxins that can harm the body. Pregnant women should watch flaxseed intake because more than 5 tablespoons a day can affect hormones and it can decrease the ability of the blood to clot. Because of the clotting factor, anyone facing surgery should stop eating flaxseed two to three weeks before that surgery.

As a food, flaxseed is often found in baked goods like bread, cakes, scones and cookies. It gives a fiber punch to baked goods making them a little better for your body. To use flax in baking, replace ½ to 1 cup regular flour with flax meal or substitute 1 tablespoons of flax and 3 tablespoons water for an egg. Other culinary ideas including sprinkling seed on fresh fruit, in cereal or yogurt for breakfast, putting it in salad dressing or smoothies. You can also make delicious dinner entrees without meat.

Flax is high in fiber and helps the digestive system move things along. It is said to lower cholesterol, improve blood sugar by blocking insulin sensitivity, reduce hot flashes for those in menopause and it helps you to lose a little weight. It is filled with Magnesium and Omega-3 fatty acids. Just make sure to drink liquids when eating flaxseed because there is a slight chance of too much seed and not enough water causing constipation.

Juniper Berry

The bitter and astringent flavor of juniper berries make them an earthy flavor. Sometimes they remind me of pine with a little fruit flavor and they are a bit overpowering, so a light touch is needed. Three types of berries are available and all grow on evergreen shrubs are blue to black and almost the same size of a large peppercorn. They are used dried or fresh. I suggest dried because they are more available and the shrubs are hard to grow. The three types of shrubs are Junipurus virgimana, Junipurus chinensis and Junipurus communis the latter being the most flavorful. The interesting thing about dried berries is that they cannot be picked when they are green and it takes about 3 years to ripen to a blue/dusty black. That is why they are expensive.

They are often called gin berries because in 17th century Netherlands, they used the berries to flavor gin. They made a drink called Julumust that was served at Christmas. Juniper berries were also dug up from Egyptian tombs and the Greeks used them as a medicine or to increase stamina. Romans ground dry berries on food like pepper.

If you get ground juniper berries, they will only last a few weeks in an airtight container. If you get whole and grind them when you need them, the berries will last about 2 years stored airtight.

Add juniper berries to marinades whole and remove the berries before eating. The berries should always be crushed or you might be missing some teeth. Put them in bread or rice stuffing or serve with apples, prunes and other fruit. The flavor goes well with wild game like bore or venison, chicken, pork, beef and salmon. Put it in some venison chili for a real treat. It tames that wild flavor of the meat. Many times, it is in prepared sauerkraut but you can always add some crushed berry at the end of cooking if you like.

Juniper berries are known for their healing of the urinary tract. Consuming tea improves urinary tract infections of any kind and encourages good digestion and discourages heartburn and stomach issues associated with eating. It is reported to help with colitis, increase the appetite, helps a cough due to cold or bronchitis and gets rid of kidney stones, sore joints and is a diuretic. It is also thought to decrease sugar levels in the blood and increase insulin production in the body.

Lovage

Lovage comes to us from Southern Europe where was used in cooking by Romans and Greeks. Kitchens in the Middle Ages wouldn't be without lovage and seeds for planting came at a price. It came to New England from Europe with settlers and the puritans chewed on the seed to keep themselves awake during long church services and they candied the roots for a sweet treat. In Scotland, lovage grows wild. The seeds, leaves, stalk and root are all used in some manner. The flavor is like parsley but much stronger and dried is stronger than fresh. There is some note of citrus or anise in the flavor as well. The herb comes from the parsley family and the stalks look much like celery. The seeds are small crescent shaped with tiny brown ridges. The plant grows 3 to 7 feet high, depending on where you are and the type and the leaves are bright green and feathery. The flower is a bright yellow green and that is what produces the seed. The seed, like parsley, takes a long time to germinate. Plant in a sunny well drained area early spring (late fall in cold climates) because lovage does not like heat. It will come back again the next year and be much more productive. Divide plants every 2 years.

Lovage is great in soups and stews or anything that is long cooked. Use it raw on salads or in sauces. Bake in bread or combine the seeds with cheese. Candy the stalks or leaves with sugar for a real old fashion treat and decorate cakes with the leaves. Old timers will often peel the root and pickle it. Use with eggs, potato salad, egg salad, salsa dips and with chicken and fish.

Lovage can ease the pain of stomach aches, cramping due to periods, sore throat, enlarged tonsils, arthritis and gas. Either make lovage tea or chew on the seed. Lovage can be a diuretic but be careful you don't drain yourself of too much liquid and dehydrate yourself. Salves are often made for skin problems and work very nicely. If you have a boil, use heated leaves as a poultice and it can make the boil reduce. Ancient Romans and Greeks used an infusion as a foot bath. Mix with equal amounts of mint or lavender and put it in as warm water as you can tolerate. Lovage is an anti-inflammatory and will help with any inflammation. If you have kidney problems, because it is a diuretic or are pregnant, since it can start menstruation, it is probably best to avoid lovage in large quantities.

Onion

Most do not consider onions an herb, but like garlic, they are used to flavor food. Onions come in many different types and shapes. Green onions are just young onions instead of leaving in the ground for a long time to develop a bulb. Onions come in white, brown, red and purple and their flavor varies on the hotness scale from a 3 to a 7. Some are pungent and some are sweet. Green onions are green on the top and white on the bottom and all but the very top of the green part is used. Bulb onions have a papery skin that is peeled and discarded. Use onions fresh or use dehydrated onion found in the herb and spice area at your grocery store. Keep unpeeled onions out of the refrigerator in a dark, cool area for a few weeks or peel and chop and put in the freezer for a few months.

The origin of onions is not very clear but conjecture dictates that they came from Asia and grew wild. There is some evidence of cultivation during the prehistoric era. Onions can be traced back to 3500 BC in India and King Ramses in Egypt thought onions to be a symbol of eternal life and had two placed in his eye sockets before he was mummified.

Grow onions in your back yard garden. Plant in spring by sets, or tiny immature bulbs in well drained soil in full sun. March is a good time to plant in cold regions. Plant about 6 inches apart. Harvest for green onions at will or wait until the stalk starts to brown to harvest bulbs under the ground. Bulbs must be cured by placing on newspaper in in a mesh bag, not touching. I use knee high nylons and place one bulb in the toe, tie a knot over it and place another onion in on top, tie another knot and tie at the top. I then hang them in a dry area, out of the sun for a week or two or until the paper skin gets papery.

Onions are a basic flavoring ingredient that emphasizes the flavor of meat and other foods. I use onions in almost everything that isn't sweet. Use with meats, eggs, beans, vegetables. Onions are used both raw and cooked. Put in salads, stir fries on burgers and other sandwiches and use in pickling. I love sweet Texas or Vidalia onions raw. I need a bit of hotter onion for cooking.

Onions have been used to make medications as well as used in cooking. Onions are antiseptic and expectorant. Make a paste out of the juice and cornstarch to heal wounds, skin irritations, insect bites and boils. Onion is reported to help with earaches and toothaches. Onions stimulate the appetite and help with digestion. They stimulate the liver and control blood sugar as well as increase bone density. Onions decrease triglycerides and thus, reduce cholesterol and protects against heart disease and clotting.

Plantain

People from Latino countries use a banana like plantain, but the herb plantain is different. In fact, some people treat it like a weed. I have some growing in my lawn. The leaves of plantain grow from a base, somewhat like dandelions, creating a rosette that have green oval and may have purplish stems and leaves. The grow about 2 inches height to 1 foot high. The leaves are rarely any more than 1 inch wide. Flowers are tiny and white that come from a thin stalk above the plant. The flowers produce seed. The parts of plantain that are used are the seed and the leaves.

Leaves taste a little like asparagus when eaten raw. It is bitter but pretty good. Never try to dry plantain. It only works if you eat it fresh. If you decide to eat plantain that is growing in your yard, make sure you and none of your neighbors use chemicals on their grass.

Plantain is native to North America, Europe and Asia and is a sacred herb to some religions. Alexander the Great used it as a medicine to cure his headaches. It is possible to grow it in the garden, but I would not suggest it since it is rather invasive and will take over. If you do decide to try and grow it, try a raised bed where the only thing in it is plantain and don't let it escape. The seed can be blown far and wide by wind, so you really must be careful.

Plantain is used like a vegetable in most cases. I put the leaves in salad and have a friend that makes chips, like kale chips, out of leaves. The seeds are good on homemade crackers, breads and muffins. When you sauté it with butter, it turns dark green and can be eaten like spinach. Put a little apple cider vinegar on it for good measure. Use plantain in soups and stews too.

Plantain is full of iron and calcium and it is antibiotic and anti-inflammatory. Rub a leaf on a wound to heal it and stop bleeding or pain. The tea is good for a cough and seeds infused in water work as a laxative. Tea from leaves is good for nausea, indigestion and will help a urinary tract infection. Use leaves as a poultice for poison ivy and other skin irritations.

Poppy Seed

Poppy seeds are definitely an earthy flavor. They are crunchy and slightly sweet and nutty with a little bit of spice thrown in. Poppy seed are tiny kidney shaped dried seeds that come from the pods of the poppy. Some say that you can come up with a positive drug screen when eating poppy seed, but you would really have to eat a whole bunch for that to happen. Poppy seed is related to the opium poppy. Black poppy seed are the types found in grocery stores but white seed also exists coming from India or Asia. It is the same flavor and used the same way. Plants are 1 to 4 feet tall with lobed green bluish green leaves that are hairy, and a white to purple flower. A pod forms on the plant after the flower blooms and the seeds are inside. I would never try to grow the poppy and extract the seeds myself when they are very available in the herb and spice section of the grocery store.

Poppy seeds have been used for many things for centuries and appear in Egyptian writings on papyrus and the seed was used as a sedative.

Poppy seeds are often used as a confectionary and sprinkled on the tops of baked breads, buns, cakes and pastries. Honey is a good sweetener for poppy seed and compliments the flavor. Put the seeds on cooked buttered noodles and pasta with white sauce. It is a great addition to coleslaw and potato salad or just sprinkle in cooked or mashed potatoes. Poppy seeds go well with cheese, curry, chutney, with root vegetables, asparagus and carrots. A filling for pastries is made with poppy seeds, butter and oil called lekvar.

An infusion of the seed will calm a cough, toothache or earache. Poppy seeds are very high in calcium, magnesium and fiber. They are great for digestion because of all the fiber. Poppy seeds are an antioxidant and help with the production of red blood cells because they contain copper and iron. Because the chemicals in poppy seeds increase red blood cells, they are also good for cognitive skills in the brain. Poppy seed contains a large quantity of zinc, which is why it is good for a cough, but also for bone health. There is something to the sedative power of poppy seed because they contain a great deal of magnesium.

Rue

Rue is not an herb most people are acquainted with. It is also known as Herb of Grace or Garden Rue and it is a low growing perennial shrub with a strong odor. It has many branches with greenish yellow leaves and greenish blue flowers. The scent of the leaves is said to make insects go far away and the dried leaves are sewn in sachets to keep bugs out of drawers. Fresh leaves and seeds are what is used in cooking. The flavor is very strong and bitter and it tends to numb the tongue. The seeds are lightly hot in flavor. It was used by the Romans as a snake bite remedy, but they also cooked it in food. It was often put in water to make it holy water, thus the name herb of grace.

It can be grown in a well-drained sunny spot but it is necessary to wear gloves when harvesting leaves and seeds. The sap can cause an itchy rash that doesn't go away easily. Dogs and cats hate the smell, so spray an infusion around the yard where you don't want them to be. Do not spray it inside the house, because it does have an odiferous tendency that is not good. I spray it on plants to get rid of Japanese beetles too.

Use leaves in salads or cook them in eggs, with fish or with cheese. In Italy they dip whole branches in batter and deep fry them then roll them in sugar. Some old Italian sauce recipes include rue in them. Some say that rue is great in beer and wine and Ethiopians make a delicious coffee with rue leaves and seeds.

Medicinally rue has been used to strengthen blood vessels including vessels in the eyes. The flavonoid rutin is responsible for that. It has also been used to eliminate parasitic worms in the digestive tract and is known as an anti-inflammatory. Rue is reported to be an adequate expectorant (tea form) and helps diarrhea and gas. It is to be avoided by pregnant women because it does have abortive properties. Those with kidney and liver problems should be very careful about consuming it at all.

Shallot

Shallots are a type of onion that is related to garlic, leeks and chives. I've always thought of them as fancy onions. The unique thing about them is that they do not look like onions once you get the brown papery skin off. Instead of being in circles, a shallot looks more like garlic and has up to six cloves. These cloves are easily chopped like an onion. The other unique thing about shallots is that they are very tender. If you cook them too long, they tend to leave their flavor, which is a mild and sweet onion taste, but the skin is so tender, it disappears. There is even a hint of garlic in the flavor of the shallot.

Shallots look like small onions and once the cloves are exposed, they are white. Each clove is rounded on an end and is flat on the other end. When a shallot is called for in a recipe, it means you use all of the cloves, not just one.

Shallots are native to the Middle East and a food staple in Egypt. Persians thought of them as a sacred herb and they made their way to Europe during the crusades. In France they love shallots and cultivate them there. Greeks and Romans considered shallots an aphrodisiac and they were banned from monasteries because they were thought to impart thoughts of a sexual nature.

Shallots need full sun and well drained soil and do very well in raised beds. Don't try to plant from seed, because it takes too long. Instead start from sets (usually 1 clove) and place in the ground with the pointed side up in loose soil. They are planted late fall, mulched over for winter with pine boughs or bark and leaf mulch and when spring arrives, they should shoot up with green tubular leaves. Move the mulch back when it gets warm in the late spring. Once the stalk browns, dig up the shallots and place them in a dark, dry place on newspaper to cure for about a week. Store them in a dark cool room for about 1 month. If you buy them in the store, they will stay good in the refrigerator about 2 weeks. If you still have more, put them in the deep freeze after chopping them up and placing in a freezer bag. This will change the texture, but they are still great in soups and stews.

The French love shallots and use them like green onions as a condiment. They make a shallot vinegar that is very good with clams, oysters and other seafood. Use shallots in stir fries, soups, salads, with rice or cook with just about any meat. Basically, use them like onions for a milder and sweeter flavor.

Shallots also have some medicinal properties, just like garlic. They are an antioxidant and rich in minerals magnesium, phosphorus and potassium. The contain B6 which boosts the immune system and B9 that helps production of red blood cells. They also contain vitamins C and A making them helpful in fighting off colds and helping with cardiovascular issues. They contain the flavonoids gulratin that strengthens capillaries and reduces cholesterol.

Summer Savory

Two types of savory exist and one is the delicate annual summer savory and the other is the perennial winter savory. The summer savory has a milder flavor that seems like a cross between thyme, marjoram and mint and a peppery aftertaste. Use summer savory dry, fresh or freeze with water in ice cube trays and keep in the freezer only to be used in soups, stews, casseroles and other cooked dishes.

Summer Savory is easily grown in the backyard garden in soil that drains well and where the sun shines about 6 to eight hours a day. Keep the plant evenly moist but not waterlogged. It will put forth pink, white or lilac colored flowers from July all the way to September and grows in bushy form about 2 to 3 feet high. The leaves are slender dark green to bronze green. Seeds germinate, or sprout, very slowly, so it is better to get plants to plant.

Romans used summer savory as a condiment, like pepper, way before it was used as a remedy or put in other foods. Romans brought the herb to England and it found a home there. The English love to include it in bread stuffing for fowl. The Romans also thought the herb to be an aphrodisiac and thus it was not allowed to be grown in monastery gardens and the Druids used it for fertility rites. During World War II there was a shortage of pepper and the Germans started using it instead of pepper. They still use it today along with pepper.

Put summer savory in bread stuffing, on turkey, chicken, duck or goose. It is also great for ground pork and sausage. The Bulgarians make a salt, pepper and summer savory mix to put on their food and it is a great herb to use for grilling. Summer savory is good with stuffed cabbage or grape leaves, with beans, vegetables of all kinds, sauces, mushrooms, tomatoes and with lamb and fish. Crush it first with a mortar and pestle to release the oils before cooking for best flavor.

Summer savory has a bunch of medicinal uses too. Rub a leaf on a bee stick to take away the pain. It has thymol, which is an antiseptic. Some say it also contains the phenol carvacrol that is supposed to prevent the growth of bacteria. It is full of potassium and iron and helps to control the heart rate and develop strong red blood cells. It also has Vitamin C to boost the immune system and strengthen the cardiovascular system. Gargle with summer savory tea to relieve and heal a sore throat of calm gas, bloat and other digestive issues. It is often called "the bean herb" because it quells the gas that occurs when beans are eaten. It is also said to help colic in babies, asthma, and arthritis.

Tarragon

Tarragon is the star of the show in French cooking, in fact, it is often called "king of Herbs" in France. It did not originate in France, instead, it originated in Siberia and Asia was first used in the late medieval period by Arabs who used it to treat snakebites and by Persians who actually did use it to flavor food. It was brought to France by the Arabs and took that country by storm. It traveled to Italy where it was given the name of "dragoncello" mostly because of its appearance having curly thin leaves that look like an oriental dragon. Thomas Jefferson is credited for bringing the herb from France to the United States where it was a little slower in popularity. It was not widely used in America until 10 years after Jefferson planted it in his garden at Monticello.

Tarragon is a perennial related to the sunflower. The herb is a bushy shrub about 2 to 4 feet high with thin wispy stems and branches bearing long thin curly leaves 1 to 2 inches long in dark green. The plant does produce a yellowish green flower on occasion but the flower is sterile and does not produce seed. Therefore, if someone ever tries to sell you tarragon seeds, don't buy them. They will not produce plants. Instead, purchase transplants or take a cutting or from an existing plant and propagate the herb in that manner.

Dried, fresh or frozen leaves are used in making culinary delights. The flavor of tarragon is bittersweet with a little note of spicy anise and it does have a distinct earthy flavor because of the hint of green grass flavor. It is pretty potent, and care must be given as to how much you put in a dish. 1 tablespoon of fresh tarragon is equal to 1 teaspoon of dried herb because it becomes more potent when dried. Tarragon is easy to grow in the garden in a sunny, well-drained area and it doesn't need much care. I usually put mine in pots near the edge because the branches will grow down and cascade over the edge. Fresh tarragon will stay good in the refrigerator in a glass of water and covered with plastic about 5 days and dried is good stored in an airtight container about 1 year or so. Hang bunches of sprigs in a dim, dry area to dry.

Tarragon is a part of the popular herb bland of Fines Herbs, a French blend. A good way to use tarragon is to steep sprigs in white wine vinegar for several weeks and then remove and strain the vinegar into a bottle. Use it in cooking wherever regular vinegar is used. Additionally, steep in olive oil and use the flavored oil in cooking. Tarragon goes well with chicken and fish but can also is yummy with seafood, lamb and beef. It is delicious in egg dishes and with many vegetables including green beans, potatoes, tomatoes, and carrots. Make a watermelon salad and put some fresh leaves in that for a real treat. I also add leaves to potato, macaroni and green salads. Use that tarragon vinegar and/or oil to dress salads.

Tarragon does have some extensive medicinal properties and the tea doesn't taste bad at all. It is a great digestive herb, so cook with it freely. It increases appetite and helps with gas. Chewing on a leaf may relieve a toothache for a little while and drinking tea may give some relief to those with rheumatism. It is known to help insomniacs get to sleep and promotes menstruation, which is why pregnant women should consume it sparingly. There are some properties in the herb that fight bacterial in the body and it contains a large portion of potassium. However, it also has a substance called stragole that can cause cancer. It also tends to slow blood clothing, so if you are taking blood thinners, it is okay to eat it but stay away from using it for any other remedy. The leaves can cause contact dermatitis for those who are allergic to ragweed and eating it can cause stuffy nose problems too.

Watercress

Some may argue that watercress is not an herb, but a leaf vegetable like lettuce. I use it to flavor other foods and add color, so to me, it is an herb. Watercress is too hard to grow yourself because it is an aquatic plant that grows in moving water and usually comes up in the spring. The only way to use it is fresh, but it can be found in large grocery stores year round. Whenever I think of watercress, I think of delicate watercress sandwiches served at formal teas, but there is much more to this plant than that.

Watercress is one of those earthy flavors that is hot and peppery. It is very pungent and used either raw or cooked. My grandmother used to steam it for a cooked vegetable but I like to add it to mashed and boiled potatoes and might even mix chopped watercress in sour cream to serve on top of baked potatoes. Try a bacon, lettuce and tomato sandwich changing the lettuce to watercress for a BWT instead of BLT. Placing some leaves in a grilled cheese sandwich lends a pepper flavor that is quite good. Sprinkle chopped watercress in scrambled eggs or an omelet or put some in Pad Thai for a pungent flavor. I have put leaves on pizza and it was very well received. Watercress either sprinkled on or steamed goes well with seafood and fish, lamb, chicken and beef. Try making pesto with watercress rather than basil and serve over noodles with some crunchy pine nuts. I have even had watercress with a watermelon and cantaloupe salad dressed with balsamic vinegar and it was divinely tangy.

Persian king Xerxes ordered his soldiers to eat watercress so they would stay strong and healthy during long marches. There is a Greek proverb that says to eat cress and learn more wit leading us to believe it is good for brain power. Watercress was used by ancient physician Hippocrates as a blood purifier and medication to treat blood disorders and it was also used to fresh breath. It was also known to cure scurvy during the 1600s.

Watercress is very low in calories; only about 4 in a cup. It is a good source of Vitamin K and C. Vitamin K is helpful to enable blood to clot well and give you healthy bones while Vitamin C keeps colds and flu away. Watercress is full of antioxidants that protect the cells of the body against damage and therefore is good for cardiovascular disease and diabetes. It has nitrates that keep blood vessels open and flowing and helps those with arthritis become less stiff. It is also said to be great for osteoporosis and it lowers cholesterol.

If you have ever been to the English countryside in the springtime, you may have encountered English watercress soup. It is a very popular dish in England with a lovely peppery flavor. It is often served with a whipped savory topping on top that will get your lips smacking for more. I put some frozen, but thawed peas in with mine after pureeing just for some texture and flavor, but they are optional.

Winter Savory

There isn't much difference between summer savory and winter savory except that winter is heartier and is a perennial, the leaves are a little glossier and stems woodier and the flavor is more pronounced. Winter savory is a semi-evergreen plant with dark green leaves and flowers that bloom in pink, lilac and white. It is used fresh, dried or frozen and grows well in a sunny area of the garden. Winter savory has the added advantage of keeping aphids and mildew away from roses and other garden plants. Many times, gardeners will use winter savory as a border plant, but it must be kept trimmed. That isn't much of a problem because the trimmings are used in great culinary dishes. The plant grows about 6 to 12 inches high and 8 to 12 inches across and stems are bundled together and hung to dry. They should keep 1 year in an airtight container. The leaves have a wonderful peppery flavor.

Winter savory is used like summer savory in beans, stuffing and with chicken, turkey, beef, lamb and other meats. It is great on the grill. It is also a favorite addition to most vegetables.

Winter savory is often used for intestinal problems like indigestion, gas, nausea, stomach cramps and diarrhea. Make an infusion and drink it down slowly. It is antiseptic and great for gargling for a sore throat or cough and it is an expectorant so it will bring everything up and out. Ointments made with winter savory are beneficial to those with arthritis. In the Middle Ages, summer savory was considered to be an aphrodisiac, but Winter savory was thought to stanch sexual desire. Those that are pregnant should not drink the tea, but it is fine to eat small amounts in food.

Moving on to chapter three, we will explore all the possibilities of herbs that give a dish dimension, definition and texture.

Chapter 3: Definition/Dimension Herbs and Spices

Herbs that give definition and dimension are those that you would notice if they were not there. Most of these herbs do not have strong flavors, with the exception of mint, but they are used often in the kitchen. Some of these herbs also give texture and color to foods. Calendula lends a nice orange yellow color and astringent flavor to food, while mustard (the seed) can be transformed into a condiment. Arrowroot might have a smidge of a flavor, but it is more often used to thicken foods that are have a lot of liquid. Aloe Vera does have a flavor and although it is mostly used for burns, it is also consumed.

Aloe Vera

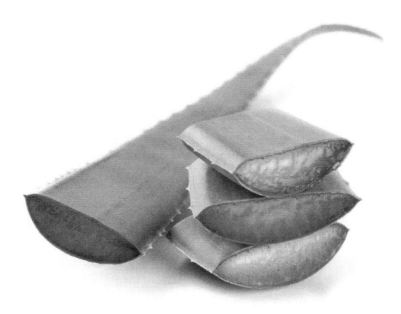

Most people know what Aloe Vera is. It is a succulent plant with big tongue-like green leaves with dull spikes on them. When you open up the leaves you have a fleshy substance with a sticky gel. The plant is also called Chinese Aloe, Burn Aloe and First Aid plant.

Aloe Vera is traced back all the way to Mesopotamia about 4000 years ago and it was also used by the Egyptians and Greeks.

The flavor of aloe comes from the sap and leaves and is fresh yet a bit on the bitter side. Many people grow the plant in pots in their windowsills. It is not a plant that can be grown outside in cold climates as it needs warm temperatures. Aloe can only be used fresh, but you can get aloe juice in most stores. You can also purchase leaves and if it is wrapped in plastic wrap and in the refrigerator, it will last a few days.

I like to use Aloe in smoothies because of all the healthy vitamins in it. Add fleshy leaves to salads or to a salsa mix to bring on a fresh flavor. Stir in soup or poach the leaves in spices. It is most often used in Latin American dishes and is always included near the final stages of cooking so it does not cook down too much. It is suggested to eat within 20 minutes of cutting the leaves because the enzymes break down quickly. Also be aware that aloe can make your tongue numb.

Health benefits are great with Aloe Vera. It is an antioxidant with polyphenols that lower blood sugar and are good for your teeth and gums. The sap acts as a laxative and can calm an upset stomach. Gargle with sap and water for a sore throat. It is good for headaches, fatigue and is also an antibiotic and antifungal. It boosts the immune system, helps with sores and skin ulcers and the gel stops the pain of sunburn like nothing else.

To fillet a leaf (you will need a large one) you skim the spikes off the sides of the leaf with a knife. Then, cut the leaf in half width-wise. Slice the skin off 1 half and turn over and remove the skin from the other side. The gel should stay together enough for you to cut it in chunks.

Arrowroot

Another name for arrowroot is aruan, meaning meal of meals. The plant produces a thick, juicy root full of starch and that root is ground down to a meal that looks much like cornstarch, however it is totally gluten free, corn free and soy free. It is often used to thicken foods and has no scent or flavor.

Arrowroot has been cultivated since 5000 BC in the Caribbean and it was taken to the Antarctic by explorers in the 19th and 20 centuries. You often find Arrowroot cookies in the baby section of the grocery store because they are gentle on a baby's stomach and few are allergic to arrowroot. It is a good "start out" food.

Use arrowroot powder or meal in stews, sauces by making a slurry and adding it to thicken everything up while simmering. Do this at the end of cooking. About 4 teaspoons to 3 tablespoons room temperature water should do the trick. Just add it to the hot liquid and stir. Don't just pour the powder into the stew because it will clump. I put some in fruit and vegetable juice to thicken them up too. Arrowroot powder works great in making gravy and it is also used as a coating when frying foods.

Arrowroot is a wonderful addition for those that are very sensitive with their digestive system. It is very gentle and also helps to stop inflammation and boost immunity. It is a wonderful agent that eases the pain of constipation and helps the body eliminate any foodborne pathogens that might cause problems. Rinse your mouth with a little arrowroot powder and water if it is sore or your gums are bleeding.

Bayberry

You have probably seen bayberry candles around wintertime. The scent is very pleasant and the flavor is different. It is astringent and tastes like bay leaves with some floral flavor. Bayberry is a beautiful shrub to have in your yard too and only enhances your landscape. It is evergreen in mild climates and will lose its leaves in winter in cold climates but come back again the next year. It grows 6 to 10 feet tall with narrow, oblong gray green leaves that are leathery and glossy. The berries are a waxy white with black freckles. Other names for the shrub are wax myrtle, waxberry, candleberry, sweet gale and bay-rum tree. The parts used are the berries and leaves and both are easily air dried or quick dried and stored in airtight containers.

Bayberry is popular with game meats because it tones down the gaminess. It works with pork roast, ribs, beef roasts and chicken and can be made into a rub or flavored salt. To make salt grind 1 ½ cup of the leaves with ¼ cup salt and store in a glass jar for about a year. Sprinkle bayberry in soups or stews or on seafood. Always grind the berries before using. In the past, bayberry was a popular thing to put in wine and rum, which gave it the interesting name of bay-rum tree.

Bayberry is an astringent and if you get a cold, it will help thin out mucous. Medications are made from the root that treat colitis, diarrhea, circulation issues and fever. Gargling with tea can help a cold and sore throat. Bayberry is a very effective mouth was as well.

Calendula

Paella is made with either fish or chicken, vegetables, rice and some spicy seasoning. The seasoning usually makes the rice yellow to orange and it tastes delectable. Calendula gives the same color as the more expensive saffron, and the flavor is different being peppery and very tangy. It gives just the right amount of zing to culinary dishes.

Calendula looks interesting in the garden too. It grows about 2 to 5 feet high with long hairy stems and oblong, toothed leaves that are green and very hairy. The flowers have a central disk, like a daisy but it is brown to yellow. The petals are yellow to orange and more resemble an aster with long thin petals coming from the disk. I like to call them pom-pom daisies. Other names are pot marigold, scotch marigold, Poor Man's Saffron, Mary-gold and Mary bud. Calendula is an ancient flower and one of the oldest cultivated. It is found in writings from the 3rd century and has been grown in England since the 1200's. Do not use calendula from a florist, because they may have been treated with insecticide.

The petals are what is used in cooking and in most other applications. The petals are used fresh or dried. I dry mine on plastic screens pulling them off the flower or I hang a whole flower by the stem in a paper lunch bag and let them dry, then pull off the petals. Calendula is very good with cheese and egg dishes and brightens the color of the food and makes it taste good too. The petals go well in salads, in soups, in cream cheese, rice and cottage cheese. I prefer fresh, but dried works too. Always remove the white ends of the petal where it connects with the disk. That part is very bitter.

Calendula tea is great for wounds because it is antiseptic and antimicrobial. It guards against viruses and bacteria. The tea is also astringent and works as a rinse on the face if you have acne. An irritated throat or cold is eased by gargling with an infusion while drinking the tea may reduce a fever or dissipate a urinary tract infection. Store dried petals in an airtight container for up to a year but be sure to store the container in a dark, dry area. Fresh leaves will last no longer than 2 days, if that.

Celery Seed

Celery seed has a fresh, exhilarating flavor. It is much like celery itself but without the crunch and big fibrous chunks. The seeds are very tiny and round with dark and light brown ridges. Celery seed is sold whole, but it is very easy to grind yourself for the most flavor, or they are sold ground, but the flavor diminishes a bit and can be bitter. I use my trusty mortar and pestle to grind whole celery seeds so the oils can infuse freely throughout the dish. It should be noted that the leaves of the celery plant and the stalk is also edible and does flavor and give texture to food.

The Greeks used celery as a medicine but the Romans used it mainly as food and Italians still use it today. Celery comes to us from southern and eastern Europe and the Mediterranean. It is grown all over the globe and is very easy to find. I have grown celery in my garden but I found out my cold climate did not allow the celery to grow flowers and seed before the cold killed it. It is necessary to live in temperate climate to get the seed.

Celery and the seed are great in soups, stocks, sauces, salads and salad dressing. The flavor isn't very powerful, but it is noticed if not there. I like to throw seed, stalk and leaves in potato salad and the seed in coleslaw. The seed gives a punch to BBQ sauce and tomato sauce. Celery is grate with chicken, shellfish, beef and lamb. The seeds are instrumental in making pickles and corned beef and they would not be the same without them. Add some seed and leaf to salsa or chutney or add to egg salad.

Romans used celery seed as a tonic and Greeks as a love potion. It is known to bring about seductive thoughts or sleep. Somehow that doesn't go together. Tea placed on a swollen limb or on a gout stricken leg may reduce the swelling. Celery has some antioxidants that may prevent aging and it relaxes smooth muscles in the body.

Chicory

I think chicory is one of the most beautiful herbs because of the bright blue petal flowers. The stems aren't all that beautiful but stately. They are square and hairy and the plant stands 6 to 12 inches tall and the leaves are narrow and oval. The flowers have a small central disk with shaggy petals mostly in blue but can be purple, white or pink too and are about 1 inch in diameter. Chicory grows on roadsides and if you ever tried to pull it out to get rid of it you would know how hard that is. The tap root is extremely long and often just breaks off to start growing again. Chicory is as determined to grow as is the dandelion. Other names for the plant are blue sailors and succory. It is native to Europe, Africa and America but also in New Zealand and Australia. The flowers and leaves are used in cooking and the root is dried and ground to be used in coffee. I only dry the flowers to use them in non-cooking projects like potpourri. The plant does not dry well and is best used fresh.

The flavor of chicory is a bit bitter and earthy like a bitter spinach. If using stems and older leaves, it is best to parboil them or you will be chewing for days. I do grow my own chicory because gathering it near where traffic goes is a little dangerous. It does grow like a weed being very drought tolerant and doesn't need much care. It will grow in the rockiest soil and flourishes but it does need full sun.

In Egypt chicory was thought to remove toxins from the blood and ancients in Egypt, Rome and Greece used it medicinally. It is often used as a substitute for coffee and in New Orleans chicory was added to coffee after naval blockades during the civil war prevented shipments of coffee to the port. They found out it actually enhanced the flavor of the coffee and never stopped using it.

Chicory leaves are used in many areas including Italy, Greece, Spain and Turkey to serve boiled with garlic as a vegetable. It is delicious mixed in with a little pasta. The reason the root is so popular with coffee drinkers is that there is a substance in it that sweetens and intensifies the flavor of sweetness. I have had the roots roasted and they taste much like parsnips. I have collected, dried and used the roots for coffee and it isn't hard to process them. You just pull them in spring or fall and use the leaves as a side dish. Wash the roots well and dry with paper towels then mince the root. Lay on a baking sheet covered with parchment paper and slow roast at 350 degrees F in the oven until they turn golden. Use a pancake turner to turn them over once during the roasting process. Once they cool, run through a clean coffee grinder and then hand mix with coffee grounds at a 3 (ground) to 1(chicory) ratio. Adjust the amounts until you get the blend you like best. Flowers and leaves are a great addition to salads adding a little bitterness and color.

Ancient people used chicory as medicine from gout and jaundice issues to gall stones. The found it useful in liver ailments and purging the body of toxins. That meant it was also a valuable diuretic and laxative. It is also said to lessen the effects of PMS and boost the ability of the body to absorb other nutrients. Some use it to stabilize blood sugar levels. The leaves are hairy and may cause a rash on some people because of contact dermatitis.

Fresh leaves and stems will stay good in the refrigerator in a plastic bag for a few days. I do not suggest freezing or drying for food consumption, except for the root of course.

Chives

Chives are indestructible, at least they are at my house. I put a small plot of chives in a pot 10 years ago and they come back, without fail every year. I have had to report them 2 times now in a bigger pot since then and it doesn't seem to matter how cold the winter gets, they still pop back up in spring when nothing else will. When I had my big garden with a large section of roses, I would plant chives as a border all around them. This kept those nasty aphids away. If I saw the little green or brown bug on the roses, I would tie a leaf of the chives to the branch of the affected rose bush and the aphids would be gone in just a day or two.

Chives are a pretty plant with long thin, tubular green leaves looking like lush grass and they produce beautiful balls of purple in a flower on a stalk. Both the leaves and the flowers are edible. I make chive vinegar by letting leaves steep in vinegar about 2 weeks in room temperature conditions. I shake the bottle every day and might add a few more leaves by the start of the second week. Then, I strain the vinegar into a pretty bottle and shove in 3 chive blossoms. This turns the vinegar a pretty pink or lavender color and I use it to cook and make salad dressing with it. Chives has a mild onion flavor and it is best used fresh, although I have dried some for winter use and it works well in cooking. The leaves grow about 12 to 18 inches tall from tiny little bulbs that look like onions situated under a thin strip of soil. It is easy to transplant them. Just pull off a hunk of the bulbs and place them where you want them covering them with a little soil. They take root quickly and start to grow immediately.

Chives are an old herb with evidence of being useful in the kitchen for about 5000 years. The herb originated in Europe and Asia and it was also thought to grow in North America before anyone brought the bulbs over from Europe.

Do not bring chives in during the winter. The plant needs a rest period in cold to rejuvenate and come back in the spring. Those living in warm climates have a trouble keeping chives alive a long time because they lack the cold snap. A friend of mine puts plastic wrap all around her pots and leaves it open at the top. She puts it in her extra refrigerator in the garage for about 1 month and that seems to do the trick.

Chives is a garnish but is also flavorful in cooking. Chives go with anything onions are good with and I enjoy them in salads and sprinkled on soups. Chicken noodle soup would not be the same without chives. I use them with most egg recipes too. They go well with scrambled eggs, omelets, deviled eggs and sprinkled on fried eggs. Make a sandwich spread with cream cheese and chives or use it like a dip with some sour cream mixed in. I love making loaded baked potatoes and use chives rather than onions to go along with the cheese, bacon and other items I stuff back in the potato. Chives go well with just about any meat too.

Chives are a good source of vitamin C making it great for the immune system and studies are being performed on chives to discover it is true that the herb helps prevent stomach, colorectal and prostate cancer. The herb contains choline and dopamine that enhances sleep, learning and memory. The herb has vitamin K for bone health and folates that prevent mood issues and depression. It contains large amounts of potassium and is antibacterial, antifungal and antiviral.

Keep leaves fresh by wrapping them in a damp paper towel in a plastic bag in the refrigerator about 2 days. Frozen chives are good to use in cooking. I mince them, put them on a cookie sheet and place that cookie sheet in the freezer for a few hours. Transfer the minced, frozen chives to a freezer bag and put back in the freezer. Dry chives in the air dry method and place in an airtight jar. Use twice as much dried chives in cooking that you would use fresh because they do lose flavor when dried.

Mint

Mint is probably the most refreshing of all herbs. It has a cool flavor due to the menthol contained in the leaves and it is sweet to tangy on the tongue. Over 16 varieties exist so there is a great deal of variety when it comes to mint. If you do grow your own, never plant two different varieties next to each other because they can interpolate and you will get one flavor or something you may not have expected. Some varieties include chocolate mint, apple mint, pineapple mint, ginger mint, lavender mint, grapefruit mint and more. Peppermint is a little hard to find, but it has the most refreshing flavor of all. Mint just keeps growing bigger and bigger year after year because it travels underground by runners and it can become very invasive, choking out every other plant in your garden. I plant mine in containers and put them on my front porch. When I did have a large garden, I would take plastic buckets, cut the bottoms out and sink the buckets in the ground up to the bottom of the rim with 3 inches above the surface of the soil. I planted my mint in the middle of the bucket and it never escaped outside.

Leaves are the useful part of the plant and they are bright green and grow on stalks about 1 to 3 feet tall. The plant does produce white to violet flowers but it is best to pick them off so the plant produces more leaves. Air dry, freeze or use mint leaves fresh in beverages and cooking. I like a little bit of mint leaves in my iced tea or lemonade. It gives extra punch to the drink. I also use it in desserts and in savory dishes as well. If you friend has a mint plant taking over their garden, just dig up a clump and plant it in a pot and you are set to go.

The Greeks would decorate their tables with the refreshing scent of mint and then use the leaves to clean the tables. Romans put mint in their baths to stimulate the body. Legend has it that the Greek nymph Menthe used to be a woman and the god Pluto's girlfriend. Pluto's wife became jealous and being a god, she turned Menthe into a plant. Pluto couldn't reverse the curse so he made her one of the sweetest smelling plants there was.

Mint goes particularly well with chocolate and in the south the mint julep is one of the favorites during hot weather. Mint goes great in a fruit salad, especially with melons and doused with sparkling apple cider. The leaves pick up a dull salad and can be infused into vinegar to make marinades and salad dressings that are exhilaratingly good. Mint is an ingredient in spring pea or carrot soup and is used in chutneys and salsas. It is even made into a jelly to be served with lamb. Add mint to vegetables, potato salad, egg dishes and with tomatoes. Mint with cream cheese as a dip or spread is also delightful. Mint flavored water is very refreshing on a hot day and you can also wipe your sweaty face with it as an astringent to get rid of grease and grime.

Mint has the ability to calm the digestive system and get rid of pain and gas. If you get indigestion at a picnic, grab a leaf and suck on it and the tummy trouble will swiftly go away. Mint is said to improve brain function and may be beneficial to those with

Alzheimer's or Dementia to a point. If you get sleepy, sniff some mint to wake your brain up. Mint cures bad breath and a bit of mint water will help a colicky baby. Mint is an antioxidant and antibiotic, which is why the Greeks wiped their tables with mint. If you get a stuffy nose, mint oil mixed in water and sniffed or a bit put in the nose will break up the mucous. A nice cup of mint tea and sniffing up the steam will do the same. Mice hate mint. I had an old house and we would stuff mint around the rickety basement windows to keep mice out. I have known others to stuff mint around the ceiling of their basement near the boards of the house and the cement block to keep them out as well.

Mustard

If you look in your refrigerator, you will most likely find a jar of some type of mustard. It might be Dijon, brown, honey or just plain mustard as it is a favorite condiment for hotdogs, hamburgers and other foods. Mustard is also considered a flavoring (herb) for food and it comes in dry form in the spice section. This yellow powder is made by grinding the seed of the mustard plant. Seed is either yellow, brown or black and it has no flavor until some type of liquid is added to it, such as vinegar, water or wine. The flavor is spicy and hot and dried is hotter than prepared mustard.

Mustard has been used for a long time but was popular in 12 century England where the seed was ground in a mortar and pestle and combined with liquid to spice up food. During the 18th century a powder from the seed was very popular as a cooking aid.

Growing mustard in your garden is possible, but you need a lot to produce mustard seed and then you have to grind it. I prefer just getting it from the spice section and it keeps for about 1 year. Mustard plants like cool weather and can be grown from seed. The plants need about 2 inches of water a week and they must flower. A pod will form and once it is brown and the leaves of the plant yellow, it is ready. Remove the pods before they bust open, put them in a brown paper lunch bag and place in a dark dry area. Shake after 2 weeks and the pod should open releasing dried seed.

Mustard has a very sharp flavor and is used with most meats. Add to salad dressing or deviled eggs or make a sauce for seafood or add to BBQ sauce for tang. I make a meat rub by toasting the seeds in a frying pan for just a few minutes that processing in a coffee grinder. The seeds get a nutty flavor. You can make your own condiment of mustard by grinding about 1 teaspoon of seed and adding 2 teaspoons of water or vinegar mixing in a glass bowl (don't use metal because it will taint the flavor) until it creates a paste.

Mustard contains magnesium, zinc, calcium and phosphorus. It also has Omega 3 fatty acids and helps blood pressure, cholesterol, heart disease, diabetes and arthritis. It is an Antioxidant and a paste is applied to wounds or on the chest to help pneumonia or chest congestion. Some may remember a good old mustard plaster when they were kids and sick with heavy congestion. Put a little of the powder in socks and put them on the feet to prevent frost bite.

Nigella Seed

Nigella seed is known by several other names including, black cumin, black sesame, black onion seed and fennel flower, which should give you a good idea of what it looks like and the fact that it has an intense flavor. It is a mixture of onion, sesame seed, poppy seed and bitterness all rolled into one. It is a very old flavoring found in King Tutt's tome but not used for cooking. Instead it was used for preservation of the mummy. It is written that Mohammed was also familiar with nigella seed using it for healing.

Nigella is a member of the buttercup family and the flowers bloom in June. Flowers produce a large seed pod that contain pear shaped white seed that turn black when they are exposed to air. The seed is either ground into powder or left whole.

Nigella seed is used in the kitchen many ways from breakfast eggs to main dishes. The seed goes well with potatoes or eggs and is particularly good in an omelet. It is baked with Naan and included in many Indian dishes including Korma, a beef dish. Whole seeds are often mixed with feta, yogurt, lemon juice and capers for a special dip for vegetables and there is a pound cake that uses the seed as well. Sprinkle nigella seed on green beans and drizzle with olive oil and lemon juice or add to roasted broccoli drizzled with the same combination of olive oil and lemon juice. Add them to salads or include with lentil soup for a special flavor.

All through history, Nigella has been a cure all. It is antioxidant, anti-inflammatory and cures skin problems, digestive issues, lowers cholesterol and is antibiotic. A little tea placed in an infected ear might help heal it and it has been given to people with pneumonia for ages. It inhibits MRSA and prevents it from spreading. Nigella seed is reported to protect the liver, lower blood sugar and calm stomach ulcers. Put some seed in a healthy smoothie and drink it down or mix the seed with honey and take a little to enhance health. If you are going to use it on the skin, test a patch first, because it can also irritate those that might be allergic to it.

Salad Burnet

Many people have not heard of this lovely and simple herb that is super easy to grow and tastes great in salads, of all things! Another name for the herb is garden burnet and it grows naturally in parts of Europe, Asia and Africa and was brought to North America and thrives there too. Thomas Jefferson brought it to the United States to plant in his garden at Monticello but it did not come into fashion until the Elizabethan Era where it was in every garden. This is not an herb you will find readily in your grocery store, so the good thing is, it is easy to grow in a container or in your backyard. It must be used fresh because it does not retain flavor when dried and it is limp and slimy when frozen. Another great thing about Salad Burnet is that it is a perennial and will come back year after year.

Salad Burnet has a light taste of cucumber and the rounded or toothed leaves come in 4 to 12 pairs on a stem to form a leaflet. The plant grows about 18 inches high and the best leaves to use are the ones that are smaller and younger. The plant grows in clumps from a central rosette and is, in fact, part of the rose family. Salad Burnet, like mint, grows and spreads with underground runners and it is hard to keep it in check if you do not contain the roots. Either plant it in a container and protect the container during the winter in cold climates or use the plastic bucket method as described in the mint section. The herb will absolutely take over the garden if you do not contain the roots from spreading. Pretty purple flowers will appear on raised spikes, but you do not want the plant to flower in order to keep it producing leaves. Just cut the flowers off whenever they appear. This is a good plant to have in drought areas because it does not need large amounts of water to stay alive.

During the Elizabethan times the leaves were used with cream cheese in tea sandwiches. It was added to tea and lemonade. Today, many make infused vinegar to make salad dressing that tastes like cucumbers or use it in soups. Obviously, throw as many leaves in a salad as you desire. It compliments egg dishes and can also be kneaded into butter to use when cooking meat. Always add Salad Burnet at the end of a recipe when subjecting it to heat as the flavor dissipates rather quickly.

The herb was used against the plague and it was also used to stop wounds from bleeding. It is an astringent and makes a cooling face wash when infused in water that is also wonderful to use on a sunburn. It is also anti-inflammatory, which explains why it calms an upset stomach or diarrhea. Steep it in water to make a wonderful mouthwash that also stops gums from bleeding.

Sweet Cicely

Sweet Cicely isn't one of those go-to herbs you always have in the kitchen. It is an interesting herb, but you must grow it in your garden to take full advantage of it. The flavor is a very mild anise or licorice flavor and it is in the leaves, stems, flowers and roots all of which are edible. The plant is a real showstopper. In the spring, when it comes back up, it produces feathery leaves like a fern that are slightly hairy and soft. Those leaves are about 6 inches to 1 foot high, depending on the environment, can grow much taller. Clusters of white flowers grow above the leaves and then seed pods grow standing straight up in the same clusters making for an unusual looking plant. The flowers attract bees and it is very important to remove the pods when they turn brown, before bursting because the seeds are good to eat both green and brown and the plant will self-seed all over the place.

Sweet Cicely has the other names of sweet chervil, myrrh and garden myrrh and it is a perennial in the celery family. It was first grown in southern Europe in the mountains. and grows wild on the slopes of Scotland and England. It is eaten raw or cooked. Grow it in partial shade for best results in evenly moist soil. The plant needs 1 inch of rain per week. The plant retains its flavor and scent when airdried.

There are studies going on to make sure that sweet cicely is safe for diabetics but the verdict isn't in yet. If you like the licorice flavor, sweet cicely makes for a lovely sweetener that can be used instead of sugar. Leaves are delicious in salads, soups and omelets while stalks can be used like celery in stews or eaten raw. The roots were used during the Middle Ages boiled and then chewed to freshen breath and give a sweet tooth a treat. It is still used that way today. Add leaves or crushed seed to fruit drinks or yogurt for breakfast for a sweetened, different flavor. Any fruit tastes sweet with the addition of some leaves. Use the green seeds in salad but always crush the black, dried seeds when cooking because they are very hard and break teeth. Use the roots like root vegetables and include them in stews or stir fries.

The root of sweet cicely has been used in medicine for quite some time. It is said to cure asthma, help digestion with stomachache and gas, reduces cough and congestion and was often used as a blood purifier. It is antifungal, antibacterial and antiseptic and a poultice of leaves heals wounds quite nicely. It is full of Vitamin A and C and an infusion applied topically is said to help ease gout.

I love rhubarb, but no one else in my house does. I make a rhubarb compote that I mix in yogurt or with equal parts whipped cream for a lovely dessert. I can freeze this compote and use as much as I like, when I want it. I have also put it in a baked pie crust, put it in the refrigerator for a few hours and served with whipped cream. There is no sugar in the recipe and amazingly the compote is sweet because of the sweet cicely, but if you feel you need more sugar, add a few teaspoons into the mix along with the honey.

Sweet Woodruff

Sweet Woodruff is a favorite of mine even though I use it more for potpourri and sachets than I do for cooking. It was an herb used more around the house. The scent is a lovely vanilla scent with fresh mown hay added to it. During the medieval period it was a strewing herb. The fresh and dried herb was scattered about the house on the floor so it was walked on to release a pleasant scent to offset the rather odiferous scents of everyday life.

Sweet woodruff is a lovely plant to have growing in shady areas of your yard. It grows low with umbrella-like star shaped green leaves and clusters of small white flowers. It grows densely and can become invasive if not kept within the borders of the garden. I had a shady tree in my yard and grew it under that tree because no grass would grow there. It flourished under that tree. Another good thing about it is that sweet woodruff is deer resistant. They won't touch it. It also repels moths and is a main ingredient in potpourri to put in bags and in drawers and closets to keep insects away. Your clothes come out smelling fresh and lovely. Sweet woodruff was often hung in churches as a symbol of humility.

In the olden days, sweet woodruff was used for liver and kidney issues and was placed in sick rooms to clear the air. Infusions were used to help heart ailments, menopause issues and cramps along with being a laxative. It is no longer used medicinally because it can cause dizziness and vomiting in some people and may cause liver damage. Use it topically as an insect repellent or to stop bleeding. It does kill bacteria on the body and other surfaces. Sweet woodruff is a main component in a traditional spring tonic called May wine. It was a popular drink to celebrate spring on May 1st and the US Food and Drug Administration has deemed it safe to consume in small quantities, especially with alcoholic beverages.

Vanilla

Some would not consider vanilla an herb or spice, but it comes from a plant and it flavors food, so it applies. Vanilla comes from a tropical plant with long greenish yellow seed pods. The plant is a type of orchid and has firm climbing stems and green leaves. It was originally found in Mexico, in fact the Aztecs and those even before them grew these orchids and used the vanilla beans as currency or presented them to nobles. When the conquistadors came, they found vanilla beans and took the orchid back to Spain and it spread all over Europe. Today vanilla is cultivated in Mexico, Indonesia, Tahiti and the place that produces the most vanilla is Madagascar.

The orchids on which the vanilla beans grow, are very hard to pollinate and the process must done by hand. A method to do that was discovered by a 12 year old slave in on one of the French occupied islands in the tropics and that method has been used ever since. If you ever wondered why real vanilla is so expensive, it is because of the hand pollination that is done 1 day after the flower opens and the rest of the process after the seed pods, or beans grow. The beans are picked at just the right time and then they are dried and must be watched and moved hourly for about 4 months. Beans must be kept in an airtight container out of the sun, preferably in a cupboard and they will last indefinitely. If they dry out, just add moisture to them and the beans and seeds inside are useable.

When shopping for vanilla, look for pure vanilla instead of the synthetic type called imitation vanilla. There is nothing vanilla about the imitation variety because it is made with chemicals related to coal-tar. Vanilla is available in several forms including extracts where vanilla is soaked in alcohol. Make sure there is no cornstarch added to extracts for best flavor. Another way to get vanilla is in a paste where the seeds are ground or in powder where the dried extract and cornstarch are mixed to make a white powder. The best way to use vanilla is from the bean. Just cut the bean open lengthwise to expose all the little black seeds and scrape them out with the back of the knife. The pod itself can be added to liquid and will infuse a vanilla flavor that can also be used in cooking.

Vanilla is used in cooking in all sorts of ways. It lends a sweet flavor to desserts like cakes, cookies, pies and ice cream and can also be used with fruit. When adding to sweet treats it is customary to cut down on sugar because the vanilla also makes the food sweet. I like to add vanilla to French toast and pancakes or to smoothies for extra flavor.

Vanilla helps to get rid of gas and relieves nausea. Just take some extract and drop it in water and drink it down. It also helps a cough and is included in cough syrup. It is thought to help with sore throats and fever too. Put vanilla on temples for a headache or apply to wounds to help them heal faster. Studies have shown that vanilla has a positive effect on those with anxiety by just smelling it. The scent also calms the nervous system. There is some proof that vanilla helps in weight loss as well.

In the next chapter we will explore exotic herbs and make dishes from around the world
including the Middle East, India, Pakistan, Mexico and Africa.

Chapter 4: Exotic Herbs and Spices

I love to use exotic herbs and spices and make world dishes. Some of the dishes I have learned to make are from India, China, Japan, the Middle East, Mexico and more. There should be no problem finding exotic herbs and spices in your grocery store, but if it is, find an international store and they will have them. Most of the exotic herbs and spices are very hard to grow in your back yard because they need special care or tropical temperatures and there just isn't enough light in the house to grow them indoors. Let's take a trip around the world and explore different flavors with the recipes that follow.

Ajwan

Ajwan is originally grew in India and used in cooking and for health. It is also called Carom seed, Omam, Omum and Bishop Weed and comes from the parsley family. The seed is what is used and used sort of like a green striped caraway seed. The plant grows about 1 to 2 feet high with feathery leaves and red flowers.

Ajwan is good for excess gas and the seed is often chewed just for that purpose. It also helps to relieve indigestion. It does slightly numb the mouth when chewing but that goes away after a short time. Ajwan is used in toothpaste and has a good concentration of thymol that is a germicide.

The flavor of ajwan is a more pungent thyme flavor with an aftertaste of anise. The seeds contain thymol just like thyme does and the seeds can be found whole or crushed. It is suggested to slightly crush them with a mortar and pestle if using whole because they are hard. Seeds will usually keep forever in an airtight container stored in a dark area away from heat. Use it sparingly until you get used to the strong flavor and if adding to a cooked dish, about 1 teaspoon is good and remember that the longer it cooks the milder it will become, so it is great in long cooking curries.

Use ajwan with beans and lentils to give them extra flavor. Sprinkle on baked breads like sesame seeds. Add to root vegetables, green beans and they go very well with deep fried foods. I like to make hot potato chips and sprinkle crushed seed into the sour cream dip for a real punch of flavor.

Amchur Powder

Many people have never heard of amchur powder and it sounds very exotic, but truth is, it is just dried mango powder. If you like mangos, you will love to add some amchur powder to recipes. Most amchur powder is manufactured in India and usually the ones that fall to the ground and are not perfect are the ones used. Mangos are a little unusual from other fruits. Most fruit rots when falls from the tree and it is not ripe yet. Mangos don't do that. They continue to ripen even though they are no longer connect to the tree. The old way of making amchur powder, which is sometimes still used today, is to peel and slice the mangos into thin pieces and dry them in the sun. Somehow, that does not sound too appealing to me, but I have been assured that they are sprinkled with turmeric and that keeps the bugs away. Another way to make amchur is to dehydrate the mango slices, but I have been told it is not as flavorful as the old way. The dried slices are pulverized and look like a coarse beige powder. The flavor is much like mango, but sweet and sour.

Amchur powder is used to add sourness to a dish and adds more acid to foods. Use it to make chutney, soup or marinades. Sprinkle on vegetables, fruit salads or add to pickle solutions. It is good to use instead of lemon or lime juice. Add at the end of cooking because the flavor dissipates when it gets hot. I particularly like it with Brussels sprouts and cauliflower, but it is also great with potatoes and chickpeas.

Amchur powder is very rich in iron. This is one of those things that pregnant women SHOULD eat. It boosts immunity and is an antioxidant. Your hair will shine and your skin will brighten when using amchur powder. It helps with digestion and prevents gas and also fights excess acid in the stomach even though it adds acid to food. It dispels toxins from the body. It is used to treat urinary tract infections and helps get rid of diarrhea. It contains a great deal of vitamin D and treats deficiency. Make an infusion of powder and water and dab on acne to stop a breakout.

Anardana

This spice is also very simple, but not as simple as dried mango. Anardana is another fruit that is dried and that fruit is the pomegranate. We always got a treat in the toe of our holiday stocking of a bright red pomegranate. My mom would put it on a plate and cut it in half and it would squirt red liquid everywhere. Inside were these lovely round seeds orbed in a red gelatinous liquid that were sour and sweet at the same time. My mom beat the back of the pomegranate with a wooden spoon and the seeds would literally fall out of it. The dried seeds look a little like dried cranberries. They are a bit sticky but not as sticky as cranberries and they can be ground.

The flavor is sweet and sour and it is a popular spice in India, Pakistan and the Middle East. There is a little crunch to it because of the hard inner seeds and these too are often air dried, but more and more manufacturers are trying to dehydrate them for safety reasons. We see the pomegranate in hieroglyphics from Egypt and this tells us that it is an old fruit. Remains were also found in Jericho and the fruit was found documented in Asia, and Africa too.

Use on barbeque ribs and other meats and on seafood. Make chutney or relish with anardana or season potatoes (especially mashed) and cauliflower. Anardana goes well with fruits but especially oranges with a little cinnamon mixed in. Put some in homemade marmalade for a real treat. Anandana is delicious with nuts, lentils and beans, chickpeas, yogurt and in breads and custards.

In the Bible it states that the pomegranate was a healing food that healed the mind and the body. I know I feel good when I eat them. Anardana contains Vitamin C and Potassium and large quantities of Vitamin K, which explains healing the mind. It relaxes blood vessels and allows the blood to flow through the body uninhibited and therefore, lowers blood pressure. It is an antioxidant and anti-inflammatory.

Asafoetida

This flavoring also comes from Afghanistan but is cultivated in India and another other names for it are Hing, Stinking Gum, Devil's Sweat or Devil's Dung. You may wonder why anyone would eat this spice and even more so if you smell it before cooking it. It is pretty terrible. Asafoetida is the ground resin from the Giant Fennel tree that only grows in India. It is an off-white to tan powder and it is a wonder why anyone got the idea to cook with this stuff when you first encounter it, but once it combines with hot fat, oil or butter a miracle happens. It smells and tastes incredibly delightful, like mild leeks or onions with a savory note. You only need a tiny pinch to make a difference in a recipe. Avoid buying a large quantity because the spice lasts about 1 year in an airtight container stored in a cool, dry and dark place. It also tends to make the spice cabinet smell if you have a large quantity of it.

Asafoetida came to Europe with Alexander the Great who thought he discovered a spice from North Africa that has a worth more than silver. It was different however but made a good substitute once that North African herb became extinct. Middle Age folk utilized it as a preservative for meat and its primary purpose was in medicine. You would have to search to find a kitchen in India that did not have a bottle of the ground gum resin because it is used regularly there. Not so much in Europe where it seemed to lose favor quickly.

Asafoetida is usually an accompaniment to meats and gives an extra savory element to the recipe. It combines with other herbs and spices like cumin, mustard seed, chilis, curry, ginger and garlic. It is delicious added to buttered potatoes, vegetables and greens. It is popular in Iran to make meatballs and in Afghanistan it is commonly used with dried meat.

Asafoetida does a great job in relieving gas problems and other stomach complains, so feel free to add to chili and other recipes with beans that produce gas in the body. It also helps digestion and an aid in breaking down fatty meats. It is also an anti-inflammatory.

Epazote

Epazote comes from Mexico and it smells just as bad as Asafoetida as evidenced by another name, stinkweed. It is also called pazolte, pazoli, and goose foot. Epazote means skunk sweat and has a petroleum-like scent but everything changes when it is introduced to heat. The plant grows wild and is cultivated and reaches about 4 feet tall with green slender, jagged leaves that come to a point and small green flowers that produce thousands of seed. The leaves are the part of the plant that is used in cooking and they can be either fresh or dried. The leaves can be frozen too. I think the herb smells and tastes like turpentine, not a great flavor at all, but when cooked tastes like a combination of mint, citrus, pine and anise. It is much stronger and should be used in lesser increments when used dry. The Mayans used epazote for medications and for cooking.

I must warn you, epazote is an acquired flavor and not many people like it the first time they taste it. It grows on you and the flavor is very hard to explain because it is a flavor all its own. You must try it. It is commonly used with beans, especially black beans in a quesadilla. I use 1 to 2 fresh leaves, chopped or 1 teaspoon dry to about 1 pound of the beans. If you add to much it will not appeal to your taste buds and can cause nausea. Add some leaves to egg dishes or to cream sauces and other dairy products. It works well in stews and is often added to cornmeal cakes and potato dishes. Add at the end of cooking for best results.

Epazote was used in the past to expel intestinal parasites in humans and animals. The tea will get rid of any stomach issues if you can stand to drink it. It is an antioxidant and does boost immunity, helps delay aging and is very good for gas.

Fenugreek

Fenugreek comes from Asia and the Mediterranean and both the seeds and the leaves are used in cooking. The seeds are so hard, they are often called stones and the leaves have a decidedly more bitter flavor. The fenugreek plant is 1 to 2 feet tall with spear shaped green leaves and seed pods that look like swords about 4 to 6 inches long with a curved tip. Each pod has about 10 to 20 seeds. I am not sure why exotic herbs and spices tend to smell terrible before they are used, but Fenugreek is no different. The leaves have a horrible stinky smell, so wear gloves if you pick them since your hands will smell odiferous for a while. The seeds are always roasted and ground and produce a yellow powder. The flavor of fenugreek is sweet, bitter and very pungent like maple syrup. It changes when cooked like a bitter burnt sugar flavor and can be overpowering.

Fenugreek is an ancient plant and there is evidence that it was used by Egyptians as a medicine. It must be planted by seed in soil that is moist and 1 foot apart. Pods are harvested when plants start to dry out and just put the pods on newspaper in a dry dark area to dry on their own. Harvest leaves any time (wear gloves).

Fenugreek is most often used in Middle Eastern food. Put some powder or leaves in yogurt for breakfast and leaves in salads. Don't use much because it is very strong. Add to soups, stews, sauces and especially sauces with tomatoes. Lemon juice will counteract an overly strong flavor. Put the ground seed or leaves in bread and it works very well with curry or in pickling spice.

Fenugreek is used to treat animals and humans for infections. It is very good for congestion as it is an expectorant. It helps with digestion issues and reduces sugar levels. An infusion is applied to skin to help inflammation of tissues.

Galangal

Other names for Galangal are Thai or Siamese ginger or zinay and it comes from Indonesia and most commonly used in Thai and Malaysian areas. It is from the ginger family and looks much like ginger. The root or rhizome is used by peeling off the hard outer skin and slicing or crushing the soft inside. The root is knobby, like ginger with the inside being white and turning yellow, then pink. The flavor is unique and very spicy yet earthy with a bit of citrus punch. Galangal should be used fresh because the dried powder just does not have the same flavor.

Historically Galangal has been used as a medication and in the middle ages it was thought to be an aphrodisiac. The most common way galangal is used today is in cooking but also in remedies. Thai soup is made with coconut milk, chicken and galangal and if you have never tasted it, you are missing out. Galangal is used in stir fries, curries, with fish and often with lemongrass and in satay and other dipping sauces.

Galangal is the go to herb when talking about inflammation. It is great to flush toxins out of the body and increase blood circulation. Tea made with the crushed, peeled root is good for digestion, nausea, motion sickness, hiccups and sunburn when applied to the skin. It is also supposed to help brain function.

Hamburg Parsley

Everyone knows about flat leaf parsley and curly parsley, but they may not be aware there is another type of parsley called Hamburg Parsley. Other names are root parsley, Dutch or German parley and it isn't the leaves that are used. Instead it is the creamy beige root that grows under the ground. Hamburg Parsley has a root that looks like a small parsnip about 6 inches long and 2 inches wide. The leaves look much like parsley leaves but are not flavorful. The root is eaten raw, like a carrot or in recipes either cooked without peeling it or dried and powdered. I prefer the fresh Hamburg parsley but it is hard to find. Germany in the 16th century was where the herb was first used into flavor food and it can be grown in your garden. Seeds are planted in early spring after soaking in water over night. The plants need full sun and well-drained soil. Once they come up, thin to 12 inches apart and mulch and the roots are ready to be harvested in about 90 days.

The roots keep fresh in the refrigerator about one week wrapped in a paper towel and in a plastic bag. The leaves are often used for garnish and will last 1 or 2 days. The root is easily steamed, boiled, pureed, creamed and served as a vegetable. Use it in stews and soups with carrots, potatoes and onions. The root does discolor if left out long, so if using in salad be sure to dip it in lemon juice so it stays white. It can be roasted with other root vegetables or put in a stir fry. Use 1 part boiled root and 3 parts potatoes for a delicious and different mashed potato dish. It goes well with beef, poultry and gives special flavor to beans and lentils.

Hamburg Parsley packs a vitamin C punch and contains iron. It stimulates the menstrual cycle when it won't start and is also a great diuretic to rid the body of excess water. Pregnant women should not eat Hamburg parsley at all. The herb is also used as a laxative that is mild in nature. Steeped water makes for a good temporary cure for earache or toothache. Because of the minerals in the herb, it is best that those with gall bladder or kidney problems avoid it.

Mahleb

Egyptians were the first known to use Mahleb and it wasn't for cooking. It was for freshening the scent of the room of the kings. It is most often used for sweet treats mostly because the flavor is both bitter and sweet, almonds like sour cherries and almond flavoring. The spice is known as Mahalabi, Marlev or St. Lucie's Cherry and is from a seed or kernel ¼ inch long with wrinkled cream colored skin. When ground, it produces a yellow powder and is very aromatic. The kernels are dried and cracked or left whole and you can grind them yourself. Whole seeds last longer that powder, which does not retain its flavor very long. Because of that it is suggested to only purchase small amounts at a time.

Mahleb is particularly good in baked goods including cookies and cakes, but it also makes a great addition to lamb tagine and cheese or milk products, especially rice pudding or crème Brule. It is also good with fruit. My favorite thing to make with mahleb is Easter bread because it has a lovely cherry-like flavor.

Mahleb does not come without some health benefits. It is probably the best thing you can use for respiratory problems like a cold, cough or congestion because it is an expectorant. Just make an infusion and drink it down warm. It also helps the body to absorb nutrients in other foods better and is helpful with digestive problems. It is also said to help brain function and is beneficial to those with dementia or Alzheimer's. The spice also calms the nerves and helps to promote a restful sleep.

Pineapple Sage

Pineapple sage is an amazing herb. It smells and tastes very much like fresh pineapple and it smelled so good, it was used in the past in Mexico to lift spirits and treat depression. Pineapple sage also is called Tamarin Sage or Honey Melon Sage and it is a perennial although in cold climates it may not come back the next year. It is a semi-woody plant with square stems (mint family) and yellowish green leaves that are oval in shape, toothed and can grow to 24-inches in diameter. Most grown in regular gardens are around 9 to 12-inches. The plant is hairy like mint and regular sage and it produces beautiful red flowers that need to be removed in order for the leaves to retain their flavor and continue to grow.

The leaves are used in recipes and remedies fresh because dried leaves do not have any flavor and diminished scent. The good thing is that even those in cold climates can grow pineapple sage in their garden or in a container. It just might not survive cold winters. The plant needs full sun and watered when the soil is dry. If the leaves are pinched back frequently, the plant will grow full and bushy.

The leaves and flowers are delicious and beautiful in salads. The flowers have little flavor but they are so beautiful, it doesn't matter. Use to make pineapple sage pesto or infuse in iced tea to get a fresh pineapple flavor. Pineapple sage goes well with fish, chicken and it is wonderful in a fruit salad. Pineapple sage enhances the flavor of melons, so add it liberally to a watermelon, cantaloupe and honeydew salad along with some strawberries and blue berries. It makes a mean quick bread and I have used it in a drink along with pineapple juice, ice, honey and Champaign.

Pineapple sage is reported to calm nerves and calm an upset stomach. It is said to lower blood pressure and ease heartburn. An old remedy is so mix the leaves with raisins to stop constipation. I don't know if that will work but I do know a cup of pineapple sage tea does calm me down on a tempestuous day.

Rose Petals

Most people do not know they can actually cook with rose petals unless they are Persian who use it all the time. I love the flavor of rose petals both in salads and cooked in breads. It is important to note to never use roses from a florist or roses that have been treated with insecticide. Also, certain roses are better to eat than others. The fancy tea rose is not a good one because of the hybridization and the flavor is not as good as the old fashion roses. It was popular to cook with roses in Victorian times so floribundas, grandifloras, cabbage roses and damask roses are the best to use. I love David Austin roses that were developed to be just like the old fashion roses. The best to use are pink, but the red and yellow varieties are good too.

Some preparation is needed to cook with rose petals. The petals must be separated from the flower head and then the white part near where it was connected, must be removed. I just use scissors to get rid of the ends. It is important to pick your roses in the morning right after the dew dries from the petals because all the oils are present in the petals at that time. Put them in a plastic bag and in the refrigerator for up to 2 days, but it is best to use them the same day. Dried rose petals are used in some recipes and they retain flavor, but it is much different than using them fresh. Just hang the flower head down inside a brown paper bag in a warm airy place out of the sun. Try not to bundle many roses together or they take forever to dry. Another method is to remove the petals, set them on a parchment covered baking sheet and let them dry there or put in a 200 degree oven for 10 minutes watching constantly. Store dried petals in an airtight container for about 6 months.

Romans used rose petals in baked goods for holidays and celebrations and in the Middle Ages they were cooked into breads and other foods as well as used as medicine. The flavor is floral, musky, earthy, sweet and sometimes citrus. The rule is, the more they smell the better they will taste. Some recipes ask to muddle the petals first before using and this is when you crush them with the pestle slightly to release oils and add to drinks like iced tea and lemonade. To make a syrup mix equal parts of sugar and water and bring to a boil. Stir in a handful or two of petals and let simmer about 15 minutes. Cool and strain the mixture. It will be sticky like a syrup. Store in a covered jar in the refrigerator for about 2 weeks and use it in iced tea, lemonade or cocktails. A hot tea is very relaxing and delicious or put ice in it to make iced tea. Candied rose petals decorate cupcakes and other sweet treats. Paint beaten egg white on the petal, dip in sugar and place on wax paper to dry. Petals and buds are nice in salads, custards, cakes and other desserts. Make rose jam, chutney, ice cream or sorbet and rose petals go well with curries and poultry.

Sometimes a recipe will ask for rose water and it is super easy to make. Just use ½ cup fresh petals in 1 ½ cup warm water in a saucepan, cover and bring to a boil. When the water has taken on the color of the petals and they have faded, about 5 to 10 minutes, turn off, leave covered and let cool. Strain and put the liquid in a dark glass bottle and store in the refrigerator. It will last about 2 weeks.

Rose petals have been used as medicine for centuries. Taking tea will help with a urinary tract infection, constipation, cleans toxins from the body and boosts the immune system. Rose petals also improve heart health, lower cholesterol, and eliminates stress and boosts the mood. They are also full of vitamin C. There is a compound in roses that speeds up sluggish metabolisms so 1 cup of tea a day can help weight loss. Rosewater applied to the face or added to the bath will help the skin glow and be soft and supple.

Saffron

Saffron is undoubtably one of the most expensive herbs and spices on the market today, but there is good reason for its expense. It comes from a flower called a saffron crocus that his trumpet shaped and has long stamens of the flower are the saffron. They look like thick red threads. Originally the flower grew in Greece, but it is cultivated today in Iron, Greece, India and Morocco and requires much care. The flavor is sweet and luxurious having a certain pungency and it has a fragrance all its own. Saffron is prepared in several different ways. The threads often come in glass tubes with a lid or stopper. They are crushed in some recipes or they are soaked for a time. For some recipes, threads are placed on a sugar cube and liquid added or a pinch is placed on sea salt and ground in a mortar and pestle. This is to draw out the flavor and the color of the saffron. Then water is added and the saffron is steeped. The water is added to the food.

Do not purchase a large quantity of saffron because just a little goes a long way. The saffron in the tube will last about 6 months and frozen, saffron will last 1 year but will not be as flavorful.

Saffron is popular with rice, with paella, in soups and stews and in salad dressing. It goes well with chicken, lamb, seafood and bouillabaisse. It goes well with vegetables like eggplant and cauliflowers and shows up in many Middle Eastern and Indian recipes. Try some with pasta or with eggs for a special treat or include it in custard. Even hot tea made from saffron tastes delicious.

Saffron also has some medicinal properties. It is said to increase mental function and memory and is being studied as a way to cure cancer. In the past it was used to calm a cough and to ease asthma symptoms. It is reported to be good for your heart and controls appetite making you feel full. Saffron contains compounds safranol, crocin and crocetn and all are antioxidant or antidepressants. It has been used to start puberty in girls and boost sex drive in adults.

Sassafras

I remember sassafras when I was very young and my great uncle used to make homemade root beer. As a kid, the flavor was really strong and much different than the commercial root beer I knew, but the flavor was intriguing and I acquired a taste for it looking forward to every 4th of July at my grandparents' home. Sassafras a North American type of tree that used to grow prolifically throughout the United States from New England's Massachusetts to Mid-western Michigan and over to Iowa, Kansas and down toward Florida and Texas. The leaves are light green and grown in lobes. Leaves or root is the part of the tree that is used. The Native Americans were the first to use sassafras, especially the Choctaw tribe. French settlers in Louisiana particularly loved the flavor and it is used in many Creole and Cajun dishes and it is called file powder where sassafras powder is mixed with other spices like coriander, allspice and sage. There is a legend that

Christopher Columbus stopped his band of mutinous sailors by telling them there was land nearby and he knew because he smelled the fragrance of the sassafras trees.

Sassafras is used fresh or dried. Leaves are ground into a fine green powder and the bark of the root is also ground into a powder. The leaves have an astringent, bitter flavor with notes of anise while the root has a woody flavor with camphor-like flavor. The USDA has considered it to be poisonous but you must consume large quantities for any type of effect. You may have a hard time buying any kind of sassafras, but I assure you the homemade root beer I drank once a year as a kid was not going to affect me adversely in any way.

Sassafras powder is often used to thicken stew and is a main ingredient in gumbo. It is great with poultry and andouille sausage and oil is made without the alleged cancer causing compound in sassafras called safrole. It is used with crawfish, okra and other vegetables and leaves are added to salads for some flavor.

The Native Americans chewed the root to help lessen a fever and Europeans settling in America used it as a pain reliever. It helps kidney stones dissolve and lowers blood pressure. Because it is a pain reliever it works well for those with arthritis and gout and a liquid calms inflammation of the eyes. It is considered a blood purifier and will relieve urinary tract infections.

Scented Geraniums

I grow scented geraniums just for their scent and because they look pretty in a pot. They are not like regular geraniums with big velvety green leaves that look like ruffled round collars and big clusters of blooms in red, pink or white. Instead they have a variety of leaf colors, textures and shapes and small flowers in white, pink lavender. Sometimes the leaves are full and sometimes skeletal. They can be all green, variegated, fuzzy or smooth or have dark or light margins around the edges, but the most magnificent thing about these plants (called pelargoniums) are the scent of their leaves. They smell like citronella and keep mosquitos away or like roses in full bloom. Other scents include lemon, nutmeg, cinnamon, mint, ginger, coconut, strawberry, orange and pineapple. The only ones I use in cooking are the rose and lemon scented ones. The others I use in potpourri.

These plants are tropical and do not do well indoors in winter as there is rarely enough sunlight to satisfy them. I treat them as an annual and get new ones every summer. There are more than 50 types with different scents and looks. They bloom June through the first part of august if you pluck the flowers off before they wilt. Scented geraniums are best propagated by stem cuttings and I usually buy the plants already ready to be put in pots. They grow about 1 to 4 feet high and in warm climates they become huge. To dry the leaves, I pick them in the morning and lay them flat on a tray covered in paper towels. The tray goes in a warm area with ventilation (my breezeway) out of the sunlight and they dry quickly, in a few days. Oven dry them by placing them on a cookie sheet covered in parchment paper and baking 200 degrees F for about 8 minutes. Dried leaves should be kept in airtight containers whole or crumbled.

Another way to use them in cooking is to candy the leaves by painting with egg white and dipping in sugar and laying to dry. Decorate cakes with them. Another cooking method is to make sugar. I use a tin airtight cannister and lay down a layer of leaves then a layer of sugar, another layer of leaves and another of sugar for as many layers as I can get. Cover and leave alone for 2 to 4 weeks. Sift out the leaves and use the flavored sugar in cooking. Scented geraniums are also used to make jelly by adding infused water to apple jelly instead of apple juice. Try some rose flavored jelly and I guarantee you will love it. The leaves are also used to flavor ice cream and sorbet or sangria, lemonade and iced tea.

One of the biggest remedies for scented geraniums is that they lift your spirits and help with stress and anxiety. I know I am always happy when working with them just because of their beautiful scents. The scented leaves are said to be an astringent for the face by dabbing on some cold tea or lift the spirits by adding an infusion to bathwater. Scented geraniums are said to ease pain, help digestion and are antifungal and antibacterial. They boost immune system, help kidney problems and heal wounds. They balance hormones that cause stress and in a 2013 West African study it was found that the tea reduces swelling and pain in joints and muscles. A tea is said to relieve migraines and headaches as well as reducing symptoms of a cold, bronchitis and bloating. They are a natural diuretic and flush toxins from the body.

Sesame Seed

Most have seen sesame seeds sprinkled on top of bread and buns but may not know they are added to many other dishes for flavor and crunch. The plant that produces sesame seed originated in India but is now cultivated in Tanzania, Sudan and Myanmar and is exported all over the world. It is one of the very first oil seed crops every grown about 3000 years ago. The plant grows around 3 feet tall with a broad base tapering to a thin top. Flowers are tubular, much like foxglove and are yellow, blue, purple and white. The flowers produce an odd looking seed pod that is somewhat rectangular with deep ridges and a beaklike hooked top. The pods, which are also called buns, are picked green and left to dry. Most sesame seeds are ivory colored, oval and flat but there are also black, brown and red sesame seeds.

Sesame seed was found in archaeological remains dated as far back as 3500 to 3050 BC and in Mesopotamia 2000 BC. The plant may have been grown in Egypt and was called sesamt.

Sesame seeds get rancid quickly so avoid buying them in bulk. They will last 3 months in an airtight container placed in the refrigerator or 6 months frozen, but frozen do lose much of their flavor.

Sesame seed is the main ingredient in tahini sauce made from roasted seeds and vegetable oil. Some recipes may call for toasted sesame seeds and you just have to put them in a clean skillet over medium heat and move them around while the brown on both sides. Add them to salads, salad dressing, vegetable dishes, soups, stews, sauces or add them to cakes, cookies and other sweets. Many stir fry recipes require sesame seeds as do sushi recipes, adobo sauce, Chinese dim sum and Cuban sesame brittle. Add to yogurt or breakfast cereal, in granola or in smoothies because they are healthy.
Use either raw or toasted if you want a little extra flavor and crunch.

Use sesame seeds for several health benefits, but I must warn you that the following benefits are predicated on the fact that you will eat 3 tablespoons sesame seeds per day and that might be a challenge. You will still get some benefit just eating some per day though. Sesame seeds are a great source of fiber and promote digestive health. They do contain compounds that lower cholesterol and have high magnesium contact making them good for lowering blood pressure. They contain Vitamin E, which may prevent plaque from collecting in blood vessels. They contain calcium for good bone help and contain substances that promote growth of red blood cells. They can lower blood sugar because they are low in carbs and high in plant protein and may boost the immune system. The seeds contain selenium and since the thyroid contains most of the selenium in the body, it boosts thyroid health. It is also said to balance hormones during menopause as it contains estrogen and may counteract hot flashes.

Shiso

Shiso is a perennial in temperate climates in the mint family that is also called Perilla leaf. Leaves and flowers are used as garnish and the leaf is dried and made into a powder to flavor food. The plant is found in India and China and was brought to Japan during the 8th to 9th century. It was also used as medications in China. The plant grows about 16 to 40 inches high and the leaves are broad, oval with a tip at one lend. The flavor is very pungent and grassy almost like a combination of basil, spearmint, anise and cinnamon. The green variety is the one most used in cooking but the purple or red leaves are used as well. There is another green variety were the leaves are slightly ruffled.

Use shiso leaves with fish, rice, tempura, soup, with veggies and with sushi. In Japan Shiso is mixed with pickles, salad and noodles and Ume Shiso is a roll made with pickled plums and shiso leaves. Shiso pares well with meat, seafood, tofu, cucumber, tomatoes, mushrooms and fruits. Sometimes the sprouts of shiso seed are used in cooking. Shiso salt is a common ingredient in some Asian foods. It is the ground leaves mixed with sea salt. Another favorite recipe is to fry the leaves in a tempura batter or pound out a chicken breast, place leaves on top and roll it, then either bake or deep fry it.   It is safe to say that any recipe that uses mint or basil can also be made with Shiso with a different flavor.

Red shiso has the same flavonoids as do cranberries, blackberries and red cabbage and those affect the nervous system and circulatory system in a positive way. Both green and red leaves are anti-inflammatory and antibacterial.   The green leaves are very rich in calcium and iron and are good for bone health, anemia and increased blood circulation. Drinking or eating shiso improves the skin and makes it look more vibrant and younger while drinking a tea may help a cold with a stuffy nose and cough. It is also known to calm nausea and vomiting and is safe to use for morning sickness. Shiso is also good to get rid of food poisoning and indigestion.

Turmeric

Turmeric is from the ginger family and it is the roots that are used in both cooking and remedies. I love the scent of turmeric with an orange/ginger flavor that is very pleasantly bitter and pungent. The herb lends a beautiful color of orange and yellow to the food too. Many use it just for the color. Turmeric is often used in Indian and Caribbean cuisine. One of the main components of the spice is curcumin, which is a good anti-inflammatory.

The plant is tropical and very pretty with large lance shaped leaves growing up from the ground and interesting spikes of shaggy white to pink blooms. Use fresh root (or rhizome) or dried powder. I find the powder much easier to find. It is possible to grow turmeric in a pot if you have a great deal of sunlight. You need a big pot because the roots grow about 12 inches down after planting a rhizome 2 inches under the soil. I have a friend with a greenhouse that was very successful in growing turmeric in a pot. She took a root and cut it in 2 inch sections with each section have at least 2 to 3 buds. She planted it in the pot with the buds up and kept the pot moist. She had 3 nice plants and was able to harvest the rhizomes and use them.

Turmeric is considered a "superfood" so making a smoothie with it seems almost natural. I use about 1 teaspoon of the dried powder in my smoothies. Add 1 to 2 teaspoons to any kind of soup, curry or stew. Add 1 teaspoon to vegetables while sautéing them in vegetable oil to give them flavor and color. I wanted my macaroni and cheese to have a golden color, so I added ½ teaspoon in and what a delicious treat that was. I also like the ½ teaspoon in rice dishes and risotto. You can even add it to pancakes or make a hummus topper with sesame seeds. Marinade chicken, fish or beef or put some in salads. Pumpkin pie, custard, or pumpkin stew is a great vehicle to use turmeric because it goes so well with pumpkin. I have even used it in scrambled eggs and in stir fries to make the color pop.

Turmeric tea is tasty and easily made with the rhizome by peeling and grating a little and boiling it in water. This is one way to take turmeric medicinally if you wish. Just adding it to food will give you benefits. Turmeric, combined with black pepper and olive or coconut oil improves the absorption of the compound curcumin, which the body does have a hard time to take in. My smoothies do have turmeric, black pepper and coconut oil along with fruit to mask the black pepper flavor. Turmeric is a strong antioxidant and fights chronic inflammation and is an antioxidant as well. It may improve brain function and Alzheimer's because it has the BDNF hormone in the brain that increases new neurons. It may also relieve depression to some extent. It is good for heart health because it makes blood move through the blood vessels smoothly and it regulates blood pressure and blood clotting. Studies are on going concerning Turmeric and cancer treatment. It is believed that the spice stops cancer from growing.

The next chapter is delightfully refreshing with citrus flavored
    herbs and spices and
includes recipes citrus flavored main dishes, breads and desserts.

Chapter 5: Delightful Citrus Flavored Herbs and Spices

I love to eat dishes that have a citrus flavor to them and there are plenty of herbs and spices that have a citrus flavor and scent. Not only do citrus flavored herbs taste good, but they smell good and some even have some health benefits. Some are lemony and some orange or lime flavored but all of them have that lovely brightness of citrus.

Beebalm

Beebalm is also known as bergamot, monarda, Oswego tea and horsemint and it is a lovey plant to grow in the garden. The plant grows about 3 to 4 feet high with green leaves that are hairy and oval with teeth on the edges that are reminiscent of mint. The flowers are what make it so incredible. They come at the top of the leaves and spew out in color looking like fireworks. Flowers come in a variety of colors including white, pink and purple, but the one to cook with comes in scarlet red. The flavor of beebalm is citrus like and the leaves and flowers are used in cooking. The flowers must be fresh but the leaves can be either fresh or dried. One of my favorite things to make with beebalm is tea with both the leaves and flower and maybe a little dried citrus peel. The Native Americans used to make tea and treated illnesses with beebalm and that is how the herb got the name Oswego Tea. I also use the dried leaves and flowers, which retain their color in potpourri. I don't think I need to say the plant attracts bees, because that is obvious by the name.

Use beebalm to make jelly and jam or mix with a fruit salad. It bakes up in breads, cakes and other desserts and is great in beverages like iced tea and lemonade. Infuse milk with beebalm and use it to make custard or ice cream. Sprinkle on lamb, fish, chicken or on vegetable salads.

Eating beebalm or drinking the tea is great for a sore throat since it is antiseptic. The herb is known to aid in stomach problems and menstrual cramps, or it can calm a cold. Use it as a fresh mouthwash and use the sap from the stems to treat burns, cuts and insect stings.

Citrus Peel

You may not think of citrus peel or zest as an herb or spice, but it does come from a growing plant and flavors food, so it may be considered one. I use citrus peel and zest in many things from

121

main dishes, to desserts and even in drinks and smoothies. It gives the dish a nice bright flavor.

Citrus fruits include oranges, lemons, limes, clementines, tangerines and more. These are all tropical fruits that grow on trees. The zest is the outer colored peel of the citrus fruit and is usually grated off. The peel is the outer colored peel and the inside white part of the skin. Use zest fresh, dried or frozen and use peel fresh or dry. Drying zest is easy. I put parchment paper on a baking pan and grate the zest off with a microplane. I then either let it air dry for a few days, covered with another sheet of parchment paper or I put it in the oven at the lowest setting with the door propped slightly open for a few hours, stirring it around occasionally. Drying peel is just as easy, but it may attract bugs. I put the peel in a brown paper bag and seal it with staples at the top. Then I punch a hole in the top and pull a string through and hang it from rafters in a dry place in my garage or in the basement. The peel dries within a week or two, depending on the humidity. You can also try to dry the peel in the oven just like the zest, but the peel needs to be cut in small pieces for it to dry in a few hours. Store fresh in the refrigerator a few days, dried in an airtight container for 6 months and frozen in a freezer bag in the freezer about 9 months to 1 year.

Use citrus peel and zest in the kitchen by putting in braising liquid for beef or in the cavity of poultry before cooking to give it a citrus flavor. Citrus peel or zest goes well with seafood, with grains like quinoa and rice and in yogurt. Place peel on vegetables before roasting them for a special treat. Make candied citrus peel to decorate baked goods and don't forget about desserts. Add to pies, cakes, cookies, cupcakes, puddings and more. Use citrus zest and peel to flavor lemonade or iced and hot tea too. Add zest to salads and salad dressing and smoothies for a bright flavor. Always add citrus peel or zest to a cooked dish near the end of cooking because the flavor diminishes with heat.

Obviously citrus peel is packed with vitamin C and calcium. It is an anti-inflammatory and contains potassium. It is known to keep blood pressure in check help with colds, runny noses and sore or irritated throat. It contains polyethoxylated flavones and those reduce triglycerides so it keeps cholesterol down. It is also thought to improve insulin sensitivity and help diabetics.

Kaffir Lime

Kaffir Lime leaves have just recently become popular in food in my area. The leaves are thick, leathery, dark green and shaped like an hourglass with two double leaves at the end of the stem. They are shiny on one said and pale and porous on the other side. They are different than regular lime leaves and have more flavor. Use kaffir lime leaves like you do bay leaves. They cook and when done must be removed. You can choke on the leaves so it is important to keep them whole and remove them before eating the food in which they are cooked. They are known as Thai Lime or Makrut lime and they come from Southeastern Asia. They are used often in Thai food.

To prepare, hold the joint between the leaves and tear them away. Roll and thin slice to make ribbons that are easily removed before eating or use whole. It is best to use Kaffir Lime leaves fresh, but you can cook with frozen ones.

Use in soups, especially Thai soups. Kaffir Lime leaves are also used in curry, stir fries, and with noodles. They are cooked with chicken, fried rice, with muscles and grilled food, with fish, in cakes and with meatballs. Sometimes you can find it in a spice paste.

Kaffir limes are a good detox tonic by drinking the tea. It helps blood circulation, skin, digestion because it is anti-inflammatory. The herb is also known to aid the immune system and help relieve stress. It is good for oral health by rubbing on the gums. It gets rid of bacteria on the teeth. It rids the liver of toxins and stimulates the digestive system. It is an anti-aging agent and used by making an infusion and dabbling it on the skin to air dry. There is a warning with Kaffir lime leaves. They can sometimes make some people nauseated. Never eat the leaves but remove them before eating or make tea.

Lemon Balm

Lemon balm is a common herb in many gardens, in fact, it kind of takes over many gardens if it isn't contained. It is in the same family as mint that propagates by underground runners. I grow lemon balm in a large container, but it also is easy to plant inside a bottomless plastic bucket in the ground that will contain the roots. Lemon balm looks much like mint too with brighter green leaves than mint that are scalloped with white flowers on top of whirls that bees just love. The scent and flavor is lemon. The lemon flavor gets weaker in heat and some people have a problem eating leaves because they are hairy and stick to your tongue. Fresh is best with this herb but I always dry some leaves to make tea.

The Greeks and Romans used lemon balm to flavor food and for medicine. Old time beekeepers would build a hive and rub bee balm on the inside to attract a new colony of bees while King Charles V took lemon balm tea daily for health reasons.

Chop leaves to put in salad or salad dressing. I enjoy vanilla yogurt with some leaves and honey mixed in. The leaves of lemon balm are lovely candied and displayed on cake as ornamentation. Just paint the leaves with egg white and dip them in sugar letting them dry a bit before using them. Make a delicious butter to use with bread and scones or drop on a steak by mixing 4 tablespoons butter with a handful of chopped lemon balm and a drizzle of honey. Mix it together, form into a log and wrap in wax paper to be put in the refrigerator until used. I like to use this butter to stir fry vegetables. Use chopped fresh lemon balm in smoothies or make a simple syrup for balmade, a mild version of lemonade. Make syrup by combining 1 cup packed of leaves in 1 cup water and 1 cup sugar. Boil a few minutes to dissolve the sugar and wilt the leaves and remove from heat and cover. Let it stand 30 minutes and strain. I store mine in a Mason jar in the refrigerator and add water and ice with a sprig added for show. Add some leaves to homemade strawberry or raspberry jam for a punch of citrus. I like putting sprigs in with cooked peas and carrots or making pesto instead of basil and serving with noodles.

Lemon balm can harm those with thyroid problems, pregnant women, children and anyone having surgery in the near future. The herb is good for nausea and it tends to calm the nervous system and anxiety. The tea is great for insomnia and is an antiseptic that is good for cold sores and wounds used topically.

Dried lemon balm is great in potpourri and rub leaves on your skin during the summer to keep bugs away.

Lemon Basil

Lemon basil is a hybrid of 2 different kinds of basil that come to us from Africa and South Asia. It is most often used in Indonesian, Persian, Thai and Middle Eastern cuisine and especially in Laos cuisine. The plant grows 8 to 20 inches tall with flower spikes. The leaves are a little narrower than those of regular basil and they have serrated edges. This plant only grows in tropical regions.

In Laos, they make a stew called "pak I tou" and lemon basil is the main ingredient. Lemon basil is good in stews too and there is a good stew called "lam" that makes good use of it. In Thailand they make a noodle dish called "khannon chin nam ya" that is delicious. Lemon basil is lovely with grilled seafood and fish or julienned over roasted vegetables. Use with zucchini, corn, bell peppers, tomatoes, beans, asparagus, eggplant, potatoes and legumes. Try with eggs and melons or in cheese. It gives a great lemon flavor to bechamel sauce and makes for a nice garnish in lemonade or iced tea.

Health benefits abound with lemon balm. The tea does wonders for a cold, fever and helps the immune system keep you healthy. It is said to aid in conception although there is no real proof of that. Lemon balm has a compound that prevents cells from dying off and it contains vitamin C. It is said to calm the nerves, lower blood pressure and make substances move smoothly through the digestive system. It also contains iron and is good for bone health.

Lemongrass

Lemongrass comes to us from India where it was used for its lovely lemon flavor and also for healing. One of its other names is fever grass, and that will tell you what it was used to heal. It is also called Phafado, Ceylon Grass, Citronella Grass and Cymbopogum.
It is typically used in Indian and Asian cooking, particularly Thai cuisine. The plant looks like big stalks of some type of grass. The stalks typically grow 1 food long, green on the outside and yellow to white inside, and are hard and fibrous. It is necessary to prepare lemongrass before using by cutting off the lower 5 inches of the stalk as this is where the flavor is. The hard outer layers are

removed and the softer stalk is cut into 2 to 2 ½ inch pieces then crushed with the side of a knife. Sometimes you must use a hammer because they are harder than normal. This is another herb that you do not eat directly. It is simmered or cooked in food and removed before eaten.

I have found cut stalks of lemongrass in grocery stores but this is hard to find in some areas. It is a tropical plant and cannot grow in cold temperatures. I usually purchase a bunch of stalks, put them in a gallon freezer bag and put them in the freezer for later use. Once I take them from the freezer and let them thaw, I prepare as normal. It is possible to find powdered and dried lemongrass but the flavor is just not as pronounced. The stalks will last 2 weeks in the refrigerator if wrapped in plastic wrap.

Lemongrass is delicious in soups and I just add it to my chicken noodle soup. However, there is a Thai soup called Tom Yung made of shrimp, chilis and lemongrass and either a clear or creamy broth that is also used to eat for pleasure or lessen the symptoms of colds and flu. Add lemongrass to stir fry dishes, beverages, or use with poultry, seafood and fish recipes.

Lemongrass is packed vitamin A and it does prevent growth of bacteria and yeast. It is known to relieve pain and swelling, reduce fever, keep blood pressure and cholesterol in check and help to simulate menstrual periods (should be avoided by pregnant women in large quantities). It is an antioxidant, antimicrobial and anti-inflammatory. Use it to stop stomach issues, headache and is a diuretic. Swish an infusion around in the mouth for oral infections. It may speed up metabolism and ease symptoms of PMS. Some people may be sensitive to lemongrass because of allergies. Always remove lemongrass before eating because it is impossible to chew and can cause bowel blockage if consumed.

Lemon Thyme

Lemon Thyme looks much like regular thyme, but the flavor is decidedly citrus. It is part of the mint family but low growing as a shrub being woody and soft with small oval green leaves used in cooking and for remedies. It tends to get woody at the base and softer with new growth. The shrub grows 12 to 15 inches high with tiny purple blooms that should not be left to bloom in order to make leaves grow and become bushy. Harvest leaves in the morning after the dew has dried and either use them fresh or hang to air dry in a dark ventilated area. Store fresh in the refrigerator about 2 days in a glass of water and store dried in an airtight container in a cupboard away from heat.

I have lemon thyme in a rock garden, but sometimes I grow in containers because the little leaves are pretty. I have also used it as a border plant and as ground cover. The plants need full sun and well drained soil being planted 12 inches apart. The soil does not have to be good for thyme to grow because it grows even in the rockiest soil. It comes to us from the Mediterranean region and is grown commercially in France, Italy and North Africa. The Greeks and Romans were the first to use the plant for cooking and health and the Greeks used the plant to incense their temples.

I use lemon thyme fresh or dried, but in soups or stews I do have some frozen in ice cube trays to use just in case I run out. Use for a fresh citrus flavor in salads or sprinkled over cooked vegetables. It can be put in a Bouquet Garni instead of or in addition to regular thyme. Use with fish, seafood or chicken for great lemony flavor. I sprinkle some on pan roasted potatoes and use in soups and stews. I have even included it in citrus flavored scones and in shortbread for an extra dimension of flavor. Lemon thyme does keep bugs away and I use an infusion and spray it on my outdoor tables and chairs.

Lemon Thyme contains calcium, potassium, manganese and vitamins A, B6, C and K. The leaves contain thymol, which is antioxidant, antiseptic and antifungal. Use a tea for bronchitis, cough and laryngitis or as a diuretic, for nausea, gas and indigestion. Lemon thyme does relax the muscles in the gastrointestinal tract, which makes it good for menstrual cramps too. That said, pregnant women should avoid large quantities. An infusion is good for itching and dandruff too.

Lemon Verbena

Lemon Verbena is my absolute favorite herb. The scent is almost overkill and the flavor is totally lemon. The plant is native to tropical South America and was transported to Europe by the Spaniards. Lemon Verbena goes by names Lemon Beebush, Lippia Louisa, Erba and Cedronella. The parts of the plant used are the leaves and they are on branches, light green in color and are up to 2 inches long, lance shaped and aromatic.

I always grow lemon verbena in the summer. It is not cold tolerant, so I plant in a pot bringing it in in late summer or early fall when it starts to get cold outside. I have friends that have been able to overwinter them in the house, but mine has always lost leaves along with 8 hours of sunlight and although they are supposed to come back as they are deciduous, mine just died. One of those friends has an operating green house and his was about 5 years old and about 5 feet high. They grow to 15 feet in the tropics. Lemon Verbena needs at least 8 hours of full sun per day and is a heavy feeder. I fertilize my pot every month with a water soluble plant food suitable for plants that have leaves used and not flowers. Only fertilize during productive months and discontinue in the winter, but keep it watered well all year round. Harvest leaves frequently or it might get out of hand. I just bundle and air dry them then put the leaves in an airtight bottle. They will not lose scent or flavor by drying.

I make many different tea blends with my Lemon Verbena leaves. Just lemon is great but sometimes I will mix Lemon Verbena leaves, dried orange peel and dried basil leaves for a nice tea. That is not all you can do with this herb. Make sorbet, ice cream and pudding or try elegant panna cotta or crème Brule. Make a simple syrup and drizzle on cakes, crepes or in yogurt. I like lemon verbena leaves chopped and included in a fruit salad. The leaves go well with seafood, fish, pork, poultry and lamb. Make pesto with Lemon Verbena leaves instead of basil and serve over hot noodles with grilled chicken breast on top. I make verbena butter by chopping the herb and adding it to softened butter, then rolling into a log and wrapping in wax paper. I cut off a hunk to put in potatoes or while sautéing vegetables and potatoes.

Lemon Verbena is good for what ails you too. It helps greatly with digestive issues including gas, nausea and baby's with colic. The herb contains polyphenols that might help you to lose weight. It helps with regulating the appetite, bloating and boosts immune system. It is an antispasmodic enabling to help with menstrual cramping. It is an anti-inflammatory and may ease the pain of arthritis. It also calms the nerves and reduces anxiety. A little tea may reduce a fever and clear congestion.

Mexican Oregano

Mexican Oregano may have the same name as Italian oregano, but it is not even in the same family. Regular oregano is a relative of mint while Mexican oregano is in the verbena family, like lemon verbena. The flavor is different too. Mexican oregano has a sweet, floral flavor with citrus mixed in, which is why it is the citrus chapter. The origin is not in the Mediterranean as with regular oregano but in Mexico where it is used in Central South America for hundreds of years as flavoring for food and for remedies. The leaves that are used grow on branches of a shrub that grows about 12 inches tall in the backyard garden and although the leaves look much like oregano leaves, they are a bit larger. The plant puts forth a flower in pink and lavender that must be pinched back in order for the plant to keep producing leaves. Mexican oregano needs full sun and will tolerate no cold temperatures. It is a perennial in the tropics but treat it like an annual in cold climates. It need space to grow as it spreads into a rather full bush. Air dry leaves by hanging stems in a warm place out of the sun and store dried leaves in airtight containers.

Any Latin-type food is good for Mexican Oregano. I put it in taco filling or taco salad, in bean soups, chili or in enchiladas. It goes well in sausage, grilled meats, baked chicken, stews and makes a mean marinade. Also sprinkle on vegetables that are baked in the oven. It gives everything a fresh, slight citrus flavor.

Mexican oregano is an antioxidant and has flavonoids that enhance cardiovascular health and may fight many types of viruses.   Tea is good for cramping during menstrual cycles, stomach pain, diarrhea and respiratory infections.

Sorrel

I love sorrel and the reason for that is the flavor and the way it looks. I am partial to the red veined variety although there is also broadleaf and French sorrel all of which are wonderful in recipes. The red leaf is the most impressive looking with arrow shaped leaves and red stems that extend to the veins of the leaves. Salads made with the red leaf variety are very colorful, but the broad leaf has larger arrow shaped leaves that are great in salads too. French sorrel has smaller green leaves and are quite nice in a salad. The plants flower in spring to summer with red to purple flowers that need to be removed so the plant still grows. Sorel does not do well any other way besides fresh, so it is a good idea to grow yourself and it is very easy to do so. It grows in full sun or partial shade and the seeds germinate in a short 10 days. The plant grows about 18 inches to 2 feet tall, depending on the variety and looks beautiful in a vegetable or flower garden. It is a perennial and will keep coming back year after year.

Sorrel was used as medicine during the Middle Ages and was grown in monastery gardens. The herb is thought to go back as far as the Ancient Egypt and Rome and was used as food. The French took sorrel to a new level and learned to cook with it and it moved around the globe. A published recipe came from Jamaica during the 1700's. It is native to Europe, the Mediterranean, Scandinavia and Central Asia.

Sorel has a very sharp citrus flavor and some varieties grown under the right conditions can even taste like wild strawberry or kiwi. The freshest flavor is in the spring when the leaves first start to grow. Sorel is used in salads raw or cooked in soups and sauces. In Nigeria they make a stew with spinach and sorrel. Sorrel is easily steamed and used as a vegetable side dish and looks like spinach but has that lemony flavor. The herb goes well with curries, eggs, goat cheese and other soft cheese, rice, fish and pasta. In the Middle East it is dipped in batter and deep fried. It is best to cook sorrel in non-metal pans or cast iron because the color and flavor change to an acidic flavor when in contact with some metals.

Sorrel can make fat more digestible, so it is good with fatty fish and meats. It is full of vitamin C and has been used to get rid of scurvy in the past. It helps with liver problems and mouth ulcers and is full of fiber. Those that have arthritis and kidney stones should avoid sorrel because it contains oxalic acid that can aggravate those conditions.

Sumac

Do not confuse the spice sumac with the poisonous stuff that grows up trees. It is a totally different thing. Sumac is a subtropical plant that is popular in middle eastern and Mediterranean cuisine. The berries that are used for cooking and remedies grow on a shrub. The berries are bright red and sumac is found ground or whole. Both should be stored in airtight containers out of sunlight. I usually purchase small amounts of the ground sumac for my use. The flavor is quite lovely. It is bright, tart and astringent and almost sour, like a lemon without the juice. Sumac was used in Europe for that lemon flavor before the Romans brought lemons to them. Many chefs like sumac because it gives food a lemony flavor without the juice.

Sumac is delicious with roasted meat including chicken, lamb, fish and beef and makes a great rub with garlic, salt, pepper and Italian seasoning. It is also great sprinkled over hummus and gives it another dimension. Sprinkle in salads to give a bright citrus flavor. My rule is to use it like paprika, so it is great sprinkled on deviled eggs, over potato salad and macaroni salad. I love it over green beans, broccoli, cauliflower or any vegetable you want to give a sour flavor. It is a component in the herb spice blend called

Za'Atar, which is often used in Middle Eastern cooking. It is possible to cut salt content of a recipe when using sumac because it adds so much flavor, you don't need as much salt. Sumac is also sprinkled over ice cream or puddings and is great in a Bloody Mary.

Sumac has been used for colds and flu for centuries. Make a tea but you may need to add some honey to it because it is sour. It is an anti-inflammatory and antioxidant. Eating some can help reduce cholesterol and blood sugar along with diminishing bone loss. A tea may help relieve muscle pain and prevent insulin resistance along with increasing heart health.

Tamarind

Tamarind is a tropical tree that originated in Africa that produces pod-like fruit with edible pulp and edible seeds. The tree grows wild in the Sudan, in India and it is cultivated in tropical areas over the world. The fruit looks like a big brown pea or bean about 4 inches long that come after a pretty yellow flower with red stripes. The pod must be manually opened or it will rot and inside are large seeds and sticky pulp. The pod curves and after removing the hard brown skin it has about 6 to 8 round balls of sticky stuff and kind of reminds me of a lumpy slug. Buy dried tamarind pods and remove the outer skin and then the strings that attach the seeds to the pod, which was the pulp before it dried. It takes a while to get pods as the tree does not produce until 7 years, but that is a drop in the bucket when the tree normally lives about 150 years.

The flavor is very tart and even tarter when the seeds are dried and ground. It is the kind of tart that makes you shiver, but it is pleasant. The pulp is sweet and tart so you only use a little and it may be a little hard to find. It is advisable to add some sugar or honey so you don't pucker up completely.

Tamarind is used to tenderize meat because of the acidity. Buy tamarind extract and use it like you would Worcestershire sauce or you can get tamarind in a paste form. Boil the pods to extract the flavor and use the infusion in recipes. The sour flavor counteracts hot flavors nicely. Use it with chicken, fish, barbeque sauce, stir fries, as a marinade, with rice and with vegetables. Tamarind is a component of Hot and sour soup that you get in Chinese restaurants.

Tamarind stops both diarrhea and constipation in a flash. It can stop a fever and help sooth ulcers. The bark and leaves of the tree have long time been applied to wounds for healing and it is an antioxidant and anti-inflammatory.

Vietnamese Coriander

Vietnamese Coriander is also called Rau Ram and it is easily grown in your backyard garden as a tender perennial. Frost will kill it and if winters are too cold, it will not return. I grow mine as an annual because it never seems to come back. It is worth planting every year though because of the flavor and because of the sheer beauty of the plant. If you want to use it in cooking, you probably should grow it, because it is very hard to find and it works much better fresh.

The leaves are pointed and narrow and green with an interesting horseshoe shape of burgundy on them. It looks like someone took burgundy paint and painted around the outside of the thumb and then placed the thumb in the center of the leaf down near the base at the stem. The stems are also burgundy.

Vietnamese Coriander enjoys full sun and it looks wonderful growing in a large pot that you can take in and protect from frost at night. It likes moist soil and does not do well in droughts. Pinch back stems frequently to encourage more growth. Store leaves in a plastic bag for about 4 to 5 days. The young leaves are more pungent than old ones.

The flavor of Vietnamese coriander is odd. It is lemony with a touch of pepper thrown in. Use Vietnamese coriander in spring rolls for a delightful and different flavor. I put chopped leaves in potato, seafood or chicken salad. It goes great with any chicken dish and in soups. It blends well with seafood and curry and is commonly used that way in Southeast Asia. I sprinkle some leaves in omelets with a little garlic and green onion and include some in fresh salsa.

An infusion of the leaves applied to the hair after shampooing will stop a case of dandruff in its tracks. The leaves are antioxidant and there is some belief that it helps lower blood sugar. Chewing a leaf or tea may help a mild stomachache and reduce fever. It is good for healing wounds and acne. Just dab an infusion on and soak swollen ankles in an infusion to stop them from swelling more. Vietnamese coriander is a good diuretic too. If you are pregnant avoid eating it as it can cause problems.

Are you a lover of hot and spicy food? If so, you will just love the next chapter full of
sensational dishes that can send smoke out your ears with the aid of some hot and spicy
herbs and spices.

Chapter 6: Hot and Fiery Herbs and Spices

I will admit that I don't normally like hot and fiery dishes, but sometimes you just need to clear out the sinuses and these herbs along with their recipes will do the trick. You will find that many of the hot herbs are used for health reasons and they do a great deal of good in the body. It is beneficial to indulge in some spicy dishes. These herbs and spices run the gambit from a little spicy all the way to red hot mama spicy and come with their own benefits too.

Cayenne

Cayenne comes from a hot chili pepper originally grown in French Guiana during the 15th and 16th century. Cayenne is the powdered form of the pepper. These peppers go back centuries being found by Christopher Columbus while in the Caribbean. He brought them back to Europe as a substitute for pepper. The peppers were used as medication and decoration long before they were used in food. Cayenne powder is made by drying the peppers on racks in the sun and then ground into powder. The seeds are always removed carefully, with gloves on because they can actually burn the skin. The peppers have high concentrations of capsaicin that give them the hot sensation. The Scoville Scale is a method of measuring the hotness or amount of capsaicin and cayenne comes somewhere in the middle of the scale at about 30,000 to 50,000.

Cayenne is used in all types of cuisines around the world and most likely in Mexican, Asian and Indian cuisines. It is used in bean dishes, enchilada sauce, rice and stir fry dishes and in curries. Add some cayenne to fried chicken or with other meat rubs and seafood. Put some with cheese dishes and eggs. Add it to your chili recipe for extra heat or with vegetables for zing. Cayenne is often used in Cajun and Taco blends. Use it anytime you want a little punch of heat to a dish.

Healthwise, cayenne is great for inflammations of any type. Use it topically for pain (be careful as it can burn skin) but just eating it can improve cardiovascular issues. It also has the tendency to clear the sinuses and stimulate circulation system. A good recipe for a cold with congestion and a cough is to mix lemon juice, honey and a little bit of cayenne mixed in. Start with just a pinch and work your way up. This will get rid of any cough; help heal sore throat and it also may boost the immune system. If you live in a cold region sprinkle a tiny bit of cayenne in your boots or shoes (always wear socks though or you can burn your feet) and it will keep your feet warm. Should you get juice of the pepper, seeds or too much generally, milk will help stop the burning. If your mount is affected, try eating a piece of plain bread to stop the burning.

Chili Powder

Chili powder and cayenne are different things and they taste different simply because chili powder has other things mixed in it. In fact, there may be cayenne powder added along with cumin, garlic powder and chili peppers and cayenne is comprised mostly of cayenne peppers. Both are on the same level at the Scoville scale but I think chili powder is a little milder and doesn't make your tongue sting quite as much as cayenne. It also has a warmer (not hot) flavor that I like better. Different chili powders are hotter than others and it totally depends on the manufacturer. Chilis were used by the Aztecs, so naturally chili powder is popular in Tex-Mex foods but also foods of Mexico, the Southwest America region, Asian dishes and Indian cuisine. I could actually write an entire book on cayenne and chilis because of all the diversity.

Use chili powder in chili with ground beef and beans or as a rub for grilled meats. Chili powder in plain old eggs makes them plain and old no more. Use with cheese, tomatoes, salsa, sauces and in barbeque sauce. Use chili powder with chicken, shellfish, sausage, pork, ribs, beef and chicken and add to soups and stews for some extra punch. Don't limit yourself to main dishes. Add to sides of noodles, vegetables and even add to desserts using chocolate. Chocolate and chili powder go very well together.

Chili powder does contain capsaicin so it also helps with the same thing cayenne does, but if used topically for arthritis it is not likely to burn the skin as much. Chili powder contains vitamin A that is good for eyesight and red blood cell formation and it contains iron. Chilis increase blood flow and may help with brain performance. It dilated the blood vessels and enhances blood pressure. It is an anti-inflammatory and can increase metabolism and immunity. I mix chili powder with water and a little olive oil and spray on my roses to keep aphids away.

Cumin

Cumin comes to us from South Western Asia and it is a popular spice in India. The whole seed is available as is ground cumin and as with most seeds, the flavor lasts longer if you purchase whole seed and grind it when you need it. It is related to parsley and the plant grows about 12 to 20 feet tall with green feather-like leaves and flowers that produce boat shaped seeds about 1/8 to ¼ inch long. The seeds have tapered edges and hair like stalks. When ground, cumin has a brown color. The flavor is sweet yet bitter and nutty and smoky with a bit of heat. Toasting the seeds brings out more of the nutty flavor. Cumin is mentioned in the Bible and was used as payment for taxes and debts. The seed is the only part of the plant that is used.

Cumin is used all over the world in the culinary world. The Dutch and French put cumin in cheese and bread. In Russia a liquor called Kunmel is made from cumin. Add cumin to chili and other Tex-Mex recipes. Put it in marinades with citrus for meat and poultry. Rub toasted cumin on beef, lamb or pork and roast. Add ground cumin to an omelet for a lovely flavor and mix with onions, beans, chickpeas and lentils. A little cumin is nice on rice our couscous and add toasted cumin to stir fries. Vegetables go quite well with cumin, so add it to eggplant, zucchini, potatoes, carrots, cauliflower and more. Mix some cumin in bread of muffin dough or add it to your pickle and chutney recipes. Sprinkle some cumin on a vegetable salad. To toast cumin, use a dry skillet and heat it over medium heat. Add cumin seed and sauté stirring constantly until it is fragrant. They will make cracking sounds, just don't let them get too brown or they will be bitter. You can use the seed whole or grind it after it is cool. It is important to store either whole or ground cumin in an airtight glass container in a cool and dry dark plac3 and it will last about 1 year.

Cumin helps digestion and prevents gas. It also helps women produce more breast milk. It stops nausea and morning sickness making it safe for pregnant women to consume. It reduces the chance of food poisoning and can promote weight loss. It stimulates the digestive system by causing enzymes to activate and it also stimulates bile to be released from the liver so fats are digested easier. It is said to help irritable bowel syndrome, lowers blood sugar and controls cholesterol.

Curry

Curry is a blend of herbs, not a single herb. It usually consists of cumin, coriander, cardamom, turmeric, cayenne, dry mustard, ginger, cloves, cinnamon and bay. Different types of curry may be different colors. some may be red because there is more cayenne in it and some may be yellow because of more turmeric. There is also green curry that have more of the green herbs in it. The flavor ranges from earthy to sweet. It is also hot because of the cayenne included and it depends on the manufacturer as to how hot it is. I find it interesting that there is no curry in Indian curry. The blend was made up by a British citizen to imitate the Indian curries, or more specifically the spice blend of Garam Marsala used in Indian cooking.

That said, there is an herb that comes from South India from a tree called the curry leaf tree. These leaves are used in cooking but it is more like bay leaf, where it is removed before eating and leaves its flavor behind. The curry leaf is glossy and green with a sharp aroma. They are bitter and sweet with a definite citrus note. They are usually fried in oil to release their flavor. It is very hard to find curry leaves, but Indian food markets sometimes carry them. They are totally different from curry powder and because they are so hard to find, the rest of this section will concentrate on curry powder.

The best way to use curry powder is to blend it with a liquid before adding it to the dish you are making. It is better infused than dry. I avoid using curry powder in Indian dishes as it really had nothing to do with that cuisine. But there are multitudes of ways to use curry powder that are delicious. I love curry powder with vegetables like cauliflower, carrots, potatoes, sweet potatoes and Brussels sprouts. I usually mix it with olive oil and apply to the vegetables. It is really good with sweet potato fries and I make mine in an air fryer mixing curry powder with the little bit of oil and salt and coating the fries then cooking them. Hummus is already wet so it is fine to shake a little curry powder in the hummus and mix it up. It gives the hummus more dimension and flavor. Curry powder works very well with chicken, crab, beef and lamb and it is a great addition to beans and lentils. It works well in tomato sauce and in rice or couscous too.

Curry powder is only as good as the ingredients to make the blend when it comes to health benefits. Look on the label and see what herbs and spices were used to make up your brand of curry powder and then look at each of the herbs in the book to see what health benefits there may be. Many of the herbs comprising curry powder are anti-inflammatory and most help the digestive tract and many also help arthritis and cardiovascular issues.

Horseradish

Horseradish is a very strong herb also known as Sea Radish. It is a perennial with leaves that grow in rosettes from the center stem and get 12 to 40 inches and are smooth or crinkled. The leaves can reach 5 fit high   It is the taproot that is used and it looks like a thick cream colored carrot that can grow 20 inches long. It is not very cold hardy and may or may not come back the next year in cold climates. The flavor is hot and that is about all that can be said about that. It is normally grated and mixed with vinegar and sometimes colored with red beet juice. It is intensely hot but a little bit sweet too.

My uncle used to process horseradish in a maple syrup barn out back of his house. You always knew he was making it because it would smell for miles. He would come out wearing a yellow slicker, hip high yellow boots, a thick woolen hat, thick rubber gloves and goggles. Just parking in the driveway near the barn made your eyes water but the horseradish was magnificent. Horseradish is one of the five bitter herbs at the Jewish Seder during Passover and ancient Greeks and Egyptians used it as a cure all.

Horseradish is an easy to grow herb and it just needs a sunny spot good drainage for water in order to flourish. It is very hard to harvest because the root is extremely long and hard to pull out of the ground not to mention that grating it is odiferous, so I would think twice about growing it in your garden. It also is a huge plant and takes up room in the garden.

Add a little horseradish to hummus for a wonderful flavor that will clear the sinuses. Use it in salad dressings or with sliced tomatoes and a little chopped basil. It goes with most fish, beef, oysters, eggs, salmon, or put in soups and stews. It goes nicely with beets, peas, broccoli, potatoes, apples and mixed into a Bloody Mary. Always add at the end of cooking time because heat makes the flavor lessen.

Horseradish is good for the sinuses and the lungs. It is an expectorant that stimulates the mucous membranes. It is great for coughs and colds too. When I get an uncontrollable cough, I just take a dab of horseradish and put it in my mouth. It chases the cough away. It reduces inflammation and is an antioxidant. It might boos the immune system and fights unwanted bacteria in the body. Horseradish stimulates bile excretion to help with digestion and keeps bowels moving. It also stimulates urination and is helpful with kidney stones and bladder infections. The proper way to take horseradish is to eat it in a recipe or as a condiment or mix 1 tablespoon with a little apple cider and honey and drink it. I didn't say it would be good, but it works.

Nasturtium

Nasturtiums are such a pretty flower it is hard to believe they are edible and have such a nice peppery flavor. Other names for nasturtiums are Indian Cress and Flame Flower. Nasturtiums are an annual and vine like in nature. The leaves are almost round and green or green and cream and the flowers are trumpet-shaped in bright cream, orange, yellow and red. They are very easy to grow and sprawls a bit. I like to put them in hanging baskets because they droop down nicely. Seeds look like little nuts and are edible only when green. The flower, stems, young leaves and green seeds are all used in food.

Plant seeds 4 to 6 weeks before the last frost in your area and keep them moist but well drained. They need full sun and hate wet conditions. Plant about 10 to 12 inches apart and they will start coming up in about 10 days. Water regularly and remove dying flowers to keep blooms coming. Only harvest as much as you can use because you cannot dry, refrigerate or freeze nasturtiums.

The flower comes to us from South America and was discovered by Spanish conquistadores in the 16th century. During the Renaissance nasturtiums were called watercress. The Incas used nasturtium leaves and flowers as a vegetable cooked and in salads and they used them for medicinal reasons.

Use nasturtiums for salads or as pesto instead of or with basil. Use them in sandwiches like egg salad and ham and cheese. Add green seed to an omelet like capers. Pickle them in cold water, salt, white wine and shallots. Put in sauces, cream cheese or incorporate with veggies in a stir fry. Stuff the flowers with a cream cheese mixture and eat them.

Nasturtiums have high levels of vitamin C and are great for colds, sore throats and coughs. Leaves are antibiotic prior to flowers. Eat some of the leaves at the onset of a cold at about 1 leaf 3 times a day. Be careful about consuming nasturtium if you are pregnant or have kidney disease. They also have substances in them that promote growth of red blood cells.

Paprika

Paprika is another one of my favorites. I have made it myself, growing my own peppers and it was easy to do, but more often I buy it in tins from the market. There is a great deal of variety when it comes to paprika. Those that have only purchased regular paprika labeled sweet, plain or just paprika are missing out. Regular paprika doesn't have a bunch of flavor. It is mainly used for the way it looks. The dark red dusting gives a point of prettiness to some macaroni salad and devilled eggs, but you might not notice flavor difference if it wasn't there. Hungarian paprika is the type I like the best because it does have flavor and a little bit of heat. Hungarians love their paprika and they have 8 grades from sweet to mild and then pungent and at the end comes the hot variety. I like one in the middle somewhere with some pungency but not able to burn my tongue off. Smoked, or Spanish, paprika is a whole different flavor. The peppers used to make this paprika are smoked over an oak fire that gives them a lovely smoky flavor. This type of paprika, also called Pimentos, comes in dulce or sweet, agrodulce or bittersweet and picante or hot. In all paprika types, red, dried peppers are ground to make a powder that must be kept in an airtight container. I keep mine in the door of the refrigerator to keep it fresh and cool and it lasts longer.

Paprika started out in Central America and Mexico used by the Indians and it made its way out with the Spanish explorers. From there it went all over all the way to central Europe where the Hungarians took it to another level.

Paprika goes with a bunch of different foods and it depends on what you are making as to what type to use. If a recipe calls for smoked paprika, don't use any other type of the intended flavor will not be the same. Plain paprika, in my opinion, isn't really good for anything but adding color to a dish. If you are looking for flavor, don't use it. I use mostly Hungarian paprika when I need something not smoked. Use it with cheese, eggs, rice or in salad dressing. It goes well in marinades and rubs or in soups and stews. Use with chicken, beef, duck and lamb. I like smoked paprika in paella or barbeque sauce or anything grilled outside. Sprinkle some in the potato or macaroni salad and on devilled eggs or mix it in hummus. When cooking with paprika, there should always be a wet ingredient in the pan (oil or water) because when heated directly in a pan, it can burn very easy and become bitter.

Paprika is good for eye health. It has antioxidants in it that prevents cellular damage to the eye from age or other health issues including macular degeneration. It enables the body to convert vitamin A into a substance good for the eyes. It also allows the body to produce blood cells and reduces the risk of heart attack. It is full of vitamin B6 that helps the body produce melatonin and aids in better sleep. It also has vitamin E and allows the body for faster healing.

Pepper

I think we take pepper for granted sometimes. It always seems to be in every home in some form or another and it is relatively inexpensive as far as spices go. I personally could not imagine potato soup without a bunch of black pepper in it and I love the fiery flavor just a little bit gives recipes. Pepper is the actual berries of the pepper plant. and it has been in existence around over 4000 years. During the Renaissance it was a very valuable commodity because it came from Asia and had to be imported, which wasn't easy back then. It was used as currency and sometimes given as a gift to the gods during ancient times. Explorers started travelling the world trying to find more inexpensive markets for some spices and pepper was one of them. Today, pepper is grown in India and Asia and Vietnam is the largest producer of pepper. The same pepper plant also produces green and white pepper and it all depends on the processing of the pepper corn. Black pepper corns are dried and turn black from the drying process. Pepper can be purchased already ground, or you can grind the pepper corns yourself, which gives you much better flavor. Ground pepper will keep its flavor about 3 to 4 months but pepper corns keep their flavor indefinitely. Keep pepper in an airtight container for best results.

Pepper is low calorie and used in just about every main dish you can think of. Sprinkle or grind it on all types of meats, seafood and fish. It is especially delicious on bacon. Put it in dressings, in eggs, in sausage on vegetables and even with fruit salads including those containing strawberries and pineapple. A Christmas cookie from Sweden and Norway called pepperkaker is actually made with pepper in it and is simple spicy and delicious as is German Pfeffernusse cookies. Pepper's flavor is hot, but earthy at the same time and it pretty much goes well with just about anything except sweets.

Pepper is not without health benefits. Pepper relieves intestinal gas and induces sweating to reduce a fever. Pepper makes circulation within the body and may increase metabolism. It helps those with colds by clearing the sinuses and getting rid of fever. It also increases urination by stimulating the kidneys. Pepper tends to break down fatty foods and meat protein better and makes gastric juices do their job much more efficiently.

Red Pepper Flakes

Red pepper flakes will put zing into any dish. They are a mixture of different red chilis including ancho, bell, paprika, cayenne and chili. The peppers are dried, pulverized and crushed and put in airtight containers to be sold. Flavor varies with manufacturer and sometimes the mix also includes the seeds, which gives more heat. Some red pepper flakes are milder than others but they all have flakes in varying shades of red, pink and sometimes orange. Make your own mix using about 50 peppers and cut the tops off and lay on a cookie sheet. Turn heat in the oven to the lowest you can and put the peppers in for about 4 to 6 hours until they are dry, but don't let them burn. Place them in a food processor to pulverize and you will have about 1 cup of crushed red pepper flakes.

A good way to use red pepper flakes instead of shaking on a pizza is to infuse flakes in oil. I use olive or vegetable oil and heat it up in a pan then steep a handful of red pepper flakes, covered overnight. Strain into a bottle and use to make pasta with olive oil, using the infused oil. Use red pepper flakes in marinades and sauces for fish, chicken, beef, pork and lamb. I like to put some in my meatloaf for extra zing along with a little tomato sauce. Red pepper flakes go very well with tomatoes. Try putting some in pickle mix, with hamburgers in cheese, gumbo and omelets. Sprinkle over vegetables or put in mashed potatoes.

Red Pepper flakes are good for weight loss because they suppress cravings for fatty and sweet foods. At least that is the claim, but I've never known that to work for me and my sweet tooth. Red pepper flakes are an antioxidant and some of the peppers used protect cells and tissues against free radicals. Red pepper flakes increase the immune system and contain beta-carotene while increasing health for mucous membranes that line the lungs and respiratory tract. They are said to protect against cholesterol and lower blood sugar too.

Wasabi

Wasabi is more known as a condiment for sushi, but it is also utilized to cook delicious meals and desserts. Wasabi is a plant that grows in mountain streambeds. It originated in Japan but today it is also grown in the United States in the Pacific Northwest and in the Blue Ridge Mountains. Wasabi is very finicky and hard to grow so it is very expensive. What everyone thinks is wasabi on the side of their sushi may actually just be horseradish and mustard mixed with a bit of green food coloring. It tastes similar, yet, if you ever have the real stuff, you can tell the difference. It looks much like a root or stem like asparagus with an elongated ball at the top and spiky things coming out of it. Traditionally it is grated on dried sharkskin and now you know why it is so expensive. The flavor is grassy and hot and it loses flavor after being ground and must be used quickly.

The wasabi you get in a tube is not real wasabi, but it tastes good and hot. This is what most people find in the grocery store or sometimes you can find wasabi powder that you rehydrate with equal parts water and powder.

If you want to give a fiery kick to foods, use wasabi paste or powder. Glaze a salmon with wasabi mixed in mayonnaise, slip some in mashed potatoes or with vegetables. Use it in salad dressing, devilled eggs or seafood, chicken and pasta salad. Put it on pizza or mix it in with some potato salad.

Wasabi has no fat and no calories, so you can eat as much as you like. (That was a joke.) It does speed up metabolism, however. It also helps upper respiratory issues including sinus problems and colds. If you ever took a big bite of wasabi, you know this is true. It will also chase away a sore throat. Eating can relieve pain and joint swelling and if you get food poisoning, it drives it out. Wasabi detoxes the body and expels toxins from the liver and digestive system. It also stops blood platelets from collecting in the veins and arteries. Eat a little every day during flu season to keep it away.

White Pepper

The difference between regular pepper and white pepper is only the color and the way it is processed. The taste is relatively the same. The reason white pepper is normally used is in dishes that would look funny with little black specks in it. Black pepper is the dried berries of the pepper plant. When processing white pepper, the berries are picked and soaked in water about 10 days so they ferment. The skin of the seed becomes soft and is removed and is white. Some say some of the "hot" flavor also comes off with the skin and they believe white pepper is less potent than black.

White pepper is used in Southeastern Asian cooking and usually added after the dish is cooked. This is the proper way to use white pepper because heating it can diminish its flavor. Use in cream soups, mashed potatoes and macaroni and cheese so that the dish does not have noticeable black flecks in it. Vietnamese soups are noted for using white pepper as is hot and sour soup. Swedish dishes, like Swedish meatballs also imbibe in white pepper. Use it in sauces, eggs, cheese dishes, salads, with tuna, shrimp and meats. I like to get my own white peppercorns and grind them because the flavor is better.

You really can't grow your own pepper berries because it takes 5 years until they actually bear fruit and seven before they start producing enough to use regularly. The vines of the pepper plant grow about 10 feet tall and produce berries that look like clusters of grapes. They shrivel to peppercorn size when they dry. Pepper berry plants do not tolerate below 60 degrees and cannot be grown in cold climates.

White pepper, like black pepper, stimulates the gastric juices in the digestive system. The improve they way food moves through and out of the body relieve things like constipation. White pepper is full of iron, manganese and fiber and considered an anti-inflammatory. White pepper also stimulates the immune system and removes toxins from the body and has been known to burn body fat.

From the hot and fiery to the sweet and sublime, the next chapter
    will allow you to
make delicious sweet and spicy dishes with herbs and spices.

Chapter 7: Sweet and Spicy Herbs and Spices

The following herbs and spices are those that are often used in desserts because of their sweet flavor, but there is so much more you can do with them. Who would think of Christmas without a gingerbread cookie or a pumpkin pie without cinnamon, nutmeg and cloves? I love the spicy flavor of anise and cardamom in desserts and hot chocolate and I sweeten my lemonade with Stevia instead of sugar. There is another side to sweet and spicy herbs that make all kinds of main dishes, sides, beverages and more. All these sweet and spicy herbs are in the darkness of my kitchen cupboard that is away from the window and away from the stove. The sweet and spicy herbs especially need to be kept away from heat and light because their oils will dissipate and they will have less flavor. Now let us get cooking some sweet and spicy desserts, beverages, side dishes and entrees.

Allspice

Allspice is the dried berries of a shrub-like tree in the Myrtle family. It is also called Jamaican pepper because the berries do look like peppercorns but punch a different flavor of spiciness with hints of cinnamon, cloves and nutmeg. I guess that is why they call it "all" spice. Christopher Columbus thought it was black pepper and brought it back to Spain with him and it took off all over the world. The shrub is only suited to sub-tropical weather, so unless you live in a warm zone, don't even try to grow it. The berries can be purchased whole or ground and both must be stored in an airtight container. The whole berries last about a year or more and can be ground in a coffee grinder or with a mortar and pestle. The ground will last about 9 months in a dark area away from brightness and heat.

Allspice is often used in desserts and beverages like pumpkin pie and mulled cider, but they are also good with meats and main dishes. Sprinkle some allspice in smoothies or in apple sauce. It is great in soups and stews. It is part of the ingredients in gingerbread and spice cakes. Allspice is often included in sausage and is good with lamb, beef and works as a part of a marinade. Pair it with dark chocolate or make chutney with some in it. I put a little in my peach jam when I make it. Use it over cooked green beans, carrots and cabbage and your kids might be convinced to eat them. The tea made from berries is very warming and delicious.

Healthwise, allspice has many benefits. It is good for bloating and gas. A poultice of berries is good for arthritis and muscle pain. The oils of the spice affect the central nervous system and help with stress.

Angelica

Angelica is an unusual herb that not everyone grows in their backyard, but they could. It also goes by the names of wild carrot, wild celery and Michael the Archangel. Apparently, a monk who prayed for a cure to the plague saw the archangel in question in a dream and revealed the cure was in Angelica. It did help a little but not completely. It is good for other remedies, however.

The plant is tall and graceful growing 8 feet tall with stalks that are purplish at the base and light green with bright green leaves with teeth. The stem does look much like celery. which are used in cooking along with the dried seeds. It is most often treated like a vegetable in cooking but in other countries, the stems are sugared and eaten like candy. The flavor is nothing like celery, it is a strong, bitter licorice flavor that once enhanced by sugar is very delicious. I don't particularly like it much without sugar, but that is my personal taste. The entire plant is useable including stems, leaves, seeds, and the root.

Angelica makes a special dish out of many food items. In the main entrée category, it goes well with pork, lamb, fish and sometimes chicken. It is often used in desserts like cakes, cookies and as candy. Angelica goes particularly well with fruits including oranges and strawberries and with vegetables, especially carrots. It can be a vegetable by boiling cut stems in water with a little baking soda. Drain the stalks and serve as a side. Candy is made by cutting stalks into 6-inch pieces, covering them with water in a pan boiling a few minutes. Turn off and let it cool completely, then remove and peel the fibrous threads off. Cover in water a second time and boil until the stalks turn a bright spring green, about 5 to 8 minutes, and drain and cool. Sprinkle some granulated sugar in the bottom of a square glass pan and top with a layer of stalks covering them with another layer of sugar. Make sure the stalks are dry before putting them in the pan. Keep layering with a layer of sugar on top, cover and let sit 3 days. Next, shake the stalks from the sugar and put back in the saucepan covering with water and bring to a slow boil until they are clear. Drain and roll stalks in sugar spread on parchment paper, put in a sheet pan and put in oven at lowest temperature for 2 to 3 hours then cool and wrap in foil.

Tea made from the leaves and seeds helps with the conditions of a cold, gas or motion sickness. Chew raw stalk for heartburn. Angelica increased appetite and can calm stress and is often used in other countries to start a stubborn period. Therefore, pregnant women should avoid it. In the Middle Ages the seed was burned like incense to kill germs in the house. The root is filled with a gummy substance that smells lightly floral and is often used as a fixative in making potpourri.

Anise

Anise is different than licorice flavoring. It is milder and sweet. My favorite things made with anise flavoring are Italian Pizzells, a flat thin cookie made with an iron, kind of like a hard crepe and Italian wedding cookies that are little pillows of deliciousness topped with colored icing. Anise is an old herb found in ancient Egypt used in making medicine and in cooking. The parts of the plant that are used are the seeds, but leaves are used medicinally. I would not suggest growing anise in your garden because it takes a field of it to get enough anise seed to actually use. The plant grows 2 feet tall and have feathery green leaves and yellow flowers that produce the seeds. These seeds are small, curved and green at first, but once dried, they turn brown and pack a punch of flavor. I like chewing the seeds to freshen my breathe. Sometimes anise is called aniseed or sweet cumin because it is a bit on the sweet side.

The alcoholic beverage anisette is made with anise as is absinth, ouzo and Samburu. The flavor of anise goes well with lamb, salmon and other fish and is delicious with cooked carrots. I like making couscous with anise seeds in it to serve with lamb. It intensifies the flavor of citrus fruits like oranges and lemons and goes well with melons too. Try making a salad of oranges, fennel and sprinkle in some anise seed. It pares well with goat cheese mixed in and served on crackers. It is popular in cookies like pizzell and wedding cookies and the Germans make a very hard rectangular cookie with picture impressions in the top called Springerle that are made with anise flavoring. My mother used to make these coolies every Christmas and the cookies must lay out open air for a few days to harden. The whole house smelled deliciously like anise for 3 to 4 days. To make your own anise extract just mix 1 teaspoon of anise seed in 4 ounces of vodka in a sterilized glass jar with a lid. Put in a cool dry place out of sunlight and shake every day the first week and then every week for the next 2 to 3 months. When it smells like anise, strain through cheesecloth to get rid of the seed and bottle the extract in a dark colored bottle keeping it away from heat in a cupboard.

Anise is very calming to an upset stomach and the scent is strong enough to get through a runny nose and clear it up and help get rid of phlegm in the throat as an expectorant. It is good to expel extra gas in the digestive system and stops diarrhea. It stimulates the appetite and eases menstrual cramps meaning pregnant women should steer clear. However, after the baby is born and the mother is breast feeding, it helps with the production of milk. It does have estrogen-like effects and stops bloating. Some people are allergic to anise and should watch for any adverse side effects.

Anise Hyssop

My grandmother always grew anise hyssop in her yard because she liked iced tea with the flavor of licorice and mint. She hardly ever served iced tea without a sprig of the herb in each glass. I also love the look of anise hyssop. The leaves look like mint and grow 2 to three feet tall and green lance shaped leaves. The lovely fuzzy purple flowers brow on tall spikes and I throw those in salads and use them for garnish. They retain their color when dried and make a great addition to potpourri.

Anise hyssop is an American herb that the Native Americans used. They Cheyenne tribe used it as a drink to lift their spirits while the Cree put it in medicine bundles. The Ojibwa used anise hyssop as a lucky charm. It is traditionally burned as incense and it is traditional to grow by the back door to protect the house against evil. It is easy to grow and grows pretty tall and looks nice against the wall of a house. The flowers attract bees and butterflies. Plant it by seed by barely covering it with soil since they need light to germinate and thin to 1 foot apart. It is a perennial and will come back the next year. Plant in full to partial sun and don't water too much because it is drought resistant and deer resistant.

Use anise hyssop in cookies, sweet breads, muffins or infuse in warmed honey for a real treat. Make jelly and add in apricot or strawberry with tit. Hot anise tea is delicious with a little bit of infused honey and it has health benefits too. Steep in milk or cream and make custard or ice cream. Anise hyssop also goes great with chocolate, especially dark chocolate.

The hot tea relieves a cough and conditions of a chest cold and is said to also relieve pain. It helps your body to sweat and get rid of toxins. A poultice may relieve the itch and pain of poison ivy. Anise hyssop is great for the digestive system because it contains limonene, a compound that neutralizes acid and is also antibacterial. Use a compress for fever and headache and put an infusion on a wound to enhance healing. Enjoy an infusion in a warm bath to get rid of pain as it is also an anti-inflammatory.

Caraway

Everyone knows there is caraway seed on rye bread and it is darn tasty. The seeds are tiny, crescent shaped with 5 pale ridges on a brownish seed. Caraway is a in the carrot family and grows 2 to 3 feet tall with feathery leaves and flat white flower heads that produce the seed. The seed is a culinary additive. The flavor is lighter than anise seed, earthy, a little peppery with a touch of citrus and fennel. The parts of the plant used are the seeds in most cases but some people use the leaves and roots like a vegetable.

Caraway is thought to be the oldest cultivated spice and in Europe it is thought to be one of the oldest condiments. It has been used for over 5000 years all over Europe, Germany, Canada, North America and the United States. During the Middle Ages they were eaten because it was thought it would keep lovers interested in each other – maybe because no one would have bad breath if they chewed caraway. Caraway can be grown, but it takes a bunch of plants to be able to get enough to use.

Of course, caraway seeds are great on rye bread, but they are also added to Irish soda bread. The Brits make a seed cake that is lovely. The seed is good in shortbread, with in an apple salad. It is not merely relegated to breads and desserts, however. Caraway is put in pickling spices or in soups, stews and curries. They are particularly good in potato salad and coleslaw. Sprinkle on a baked sweet potato or in tomato based and potato soup for some flavor. The Hungarians put it in beef goulash and caraway is often included in make kielbasa. Sprinkle some on a pork roast or chops for a real treat or sprinkle in with cooked cabbage and carrots. Often a recipe will require toasted caraway seeds and that is very easy to do. Just put a skillet over medium high heat and add the seeds. Keep stirring about 2 to 3 minutes and remove from the heat to cool. That is all you must do.

Caraway seeds do get rid of bad breath but they also fight microbes and are antibacterial. They are thought to prevent salmonella. They contain high amounts of zinc that can help bone density and also get rid of a cold and cough. The also contain a great deal of magnesium and may help you to get to sleep.

Cardamom

Cardamom is from the ginger family and grows from a rhizome producing 10 to 20 dark green stalks with leaves and flowers that droop down. The plant gets about 15 feet tall and produces pods that hang down and inside or seeds that are used in cooking. The green seeds taste a bit sweet with a little pine flavor and the black taste like mint that has been smoked. All in all, cardamom tastes like ginger, lemon, mint and cinnamon all rolled together. The seed and pods are used in cooking and the ground type does not last long while whole seeds may be ground and last much longer. The spice has been around about 4000 years and were used to embalm mummies in Egypt. Romans and Greeks used it for perfume and the Vikings brought it to Scandinavia who took eating cardamom to another level.

The seeds are usually ground into foods and if pods are used, they must be removed before eating or can cause real digestive issues. A little goes a long way with cardamom as it is a strong flavor. It is grown in the Middle East, Asia Madagascar and India. Scandinavians love to use it on sweet rolls and breads but also include it in meat dishes. Adding the pods to rice while cooking gives it a lovely flavor. I use basmati rice and always remove the pods after cooking. Include it in cornbread, apple pie, banana bread and pumpkin pie. Mulled hot cider would not be the same without a pod included. Marinate fish and other meats with cardamom infusions or include seeds in sweet potato dishes, mashed potatoes and other root vegetables. Add a little to coffee for a European flavored treat.

Cardamom is good for bloating and digestive issues. It helps with excess gas and prevents the feeling of eating too much. It is known to help symptoms of gall bladder and help painful menstruation. It is an expectorant and helps during a cold and also gets the blood flowing better throughout the body. It is antibacterial and antispasmodic.

Cinnamon

Normally, when you think of cinnamon you may think of spicy and sweet Christmas cookies or pumpkin pie. Cinnamon quick breads may also come to mind but cinnamon is also delicious in many savory dishes giving them a warm spicy flavor that can't be beat. Cinnamon can't be grown in your back yard. Instead you must purchase it either ground or in sticks. It is the bark of the Cassia tree and there are over 100 varieties from which to choose, although there isn't much choice in grocery stores. Ceylon cinnamon is from Sri Lanka is not too dark in color and a little more delicate than other types with a hint of citrus in the spicy flavor. It is also called Cassia or Chines Cinnamon and grown also in China and South America. Saigon Cinnamon comes from Vietnam and sweeter with a bright red appearance. These are the two most common varieties found in the United States and Ceylon is the more expensive. Most cinnamon is ground or hand rolled and dried into what are called sticks or quills. The flavor is warm and spicy and needs to mix with other spices and sugars in order to actually taste good.

Cinnamon was used in Ancient Egypt, Greece and Rome and was a prized possession. They used it in foods, as perfume and as medications. In the Song of Solomon in the Bible, verses tell of spices and refer to cinnamon while in Exodus cinnamon is used as an anointing oil. The spice was one of the first commodities for trading and in the Middle Ages traders pretended there to be a scarcity to drive up the prize. They actually hid the fact that the trees were also found in Sri Lanka so they could jack up the price.

Cinnamon is good with a combination of other spices including nutmeg, cloves, ginger and allspice. It enhances flavor of cookies, cakes, pies, pudding and ice cream. It is also used in savory dishes including soups, chutneys, curries, sauces and is even in catsup. Cinnamon is delicious with fruits and vegetables including applesauce, green beans, beets, and potatoes. It pares well with poultry and fish and makes for a good marinade. Cinnamon is included in hot drinks like cider, coffee, tea and hot cocoa to give it kick. Try adding to cream cheese icing on sweet rolls or make s fruit salad and sprinkle on some cinnamon and sugar. Cinnamon is great on cereal or in granola and oatmeal for breakfast not to mention mixed with sugar and sprinkled on buttered toast. Mix with honey and drizzle over a bowl of strawberries or bananas. Use with baked squash and carrots or eggplant.

Cinnamon is anti-inflammatory and antimicrobial. Essential oils are used in aromatherapy. Consumption of cinnamon may lower blood sugar because it slows the rate at which the stomach empties and evens out blood sugar improving the body's sensitivity to insulin. It also helps with cholesterol, helps digestive problems and it may boost brain activities just by smelling it.

Cloves

Cloves are an aromatic spice usually used with cinnamon, nutmeg, ginger and allspice. The clove tree is an evergreen and cloves grow on those trees forming first as pretty pink flowers. Cloves are very hard and should never be put in anything whole and just left there. The clove is round with a head and has a short stem. They are very hard and can break teeth. The tree is a tropical tree and cloves are grown in Sri Lanka, India, Pakistan, Madagascar and Zanzibar. The spice has been used in Asian, Indian and Middle Eastern areas for about 2000 years. In the Middle Ages, cloves were used to mask smell and flavor of poorly preserved foods. During ancient times they were used as perfume and medications. In China, the Emperor would now allow anyone to visit that did not first suck on some cloves to clean their breath.

The flavor of close is very warm and spicy yet bitter and it is extremely aromatic. Cloves should be used sparingly because it can easily overpower a dish. The buds are dried whole or ground and the whole cloves keep their flavor and aroma longer.

Use cloves with meats and stews. Mole sauce has cloves in it as does mulled cider. Use cloves in breads, with cheese or with vegetables including cauliflower, broccoli, and cabbage to give them a kick of flavor. Some brands of BBQ sauce just wouldn't be the same without spicy cloves. Try making a spice cake out of a yellow cake mix by adding 2 teaspoons of ground cloves. Put ground cloves in rice, in curry and add to fruits like pears and apples. Make cakes, pies, puddings and more desserts with cloves.

Cloves have a compound in them called eugenol that is an anti-inflammatory. It helps digestive tract problems. They are anesthetic and antibacterial. A little clove oil on a painful tooth will stop the pain temporarily. Clove tea will calm an upset stomach and get rid of excess gas, diarrhea and nausea and it is a mild sedative. Sore throats are eased by a warm infusion.

Cocoa Powder

Some may not think of cocoa powder as a spice but it does flavor food and it comes from a plant, so it qualifies. Cocoa powder is a blend of different things including cocoa seed from a cocoa tree. There are many different types of cocoa powder that use different items in them. Some blends use Dutch chocolate, some dark chocolate and some milk chocolate, but there are many more varieties. Cocoa powder is made by crushing cocoa beans and extracting the fat. I always use unsweetened cocoa powder and add sweetener myself if I want it. Cocoa powder has the chocolate flavor. Unsweetened powder and Dutch cocoa is alkalized to neutralize the acidity in the chocolate. Dutch has a more mellow flavor while natural cocoa powder has the acidity and is darker in color. A warning: If a recipe does not ask for baking powder, do not use natural cocoa but use Dutch instead.

The Maya Indians were the first to use cocoa as they grew it in their region and then it was brought by the Spanish conquistadores to Europe. During the 16th century cocoa was used as a medicine that no one probably refused.

Put cocoa powder in oatmeal or pancakes and in shakes and smoothies for breakfast. Cocoa goes well with meats (beef and pork) as a rub and poultry in a sauce and is especially good in Mexican Mole sauce. Use a little in soup and in chili, in fact cocoa goes very well with anything hot including hot peppers and hot sauce. Use in candy, puddings, cakes, cookies and even pie. Sprinkle some cocoa powder over fresh fruit salad or use with peanut butter in granola bars. I know people that put cocoa powder in their coffee.

Cocoa powder can be healthy. It contains polyphenols, which are antioxidant and flavanols that are anti-inflammatory. These flavanols help lower high blood pressure and lower nitric oxide levels in the blood. Because blood pressure is more under control, cocoa is said to prevent heart attack and stroke and it relaxes and dilates the blood vessels. It also reduces bad cholesterol and improves brain function as blood flows better. Cocoa is also known to improve depression and mood because it contains tryptophan. It may even improve blood sugar levels with moderation and without a bunch of sweeteners. Cocoa reduces the appetite and may decrease cavities and gum disease.

Coriander

Coriander is the more mature part of cilantro and they are not the same thing, but from the same plant. The flavor of coriander is sweet, earthy, a bit on the citrus side and much stronger than cilantro. Coriander are the dried fruits of the cilantro flowers. The whole fruit is cracked and works well with rubs and chunky foods while the powder works better for things that are smooth. Coriander was originally used in India, Thailand, South America and the Middle East and has been around since 5000 BC. Egyptians, Romans and Greeks all used coriander in meats because it was strong and masked taste of decay. In the Middle Ages, coriander was used to mask the taste of medicine and as a medicine itself.

Coriander is used in both sweet and spicy dishes. Toast seeds to get the most flavor out of them just in a plain skillet or with a little olive oil. Put in curry, in soups, chutneys or in pickle recipes. Sprinkle over salads and over roasted potatoes or carrots. Put ground coriander in breads, pancakes, scones and in gingerbread. Add some to cream cheese and spread on a bagel for a real treat. Coriander is a good addition to marinade for meats or in gravies. It goes well with mushrooms, spinach, potatoes, sprinkled on sweet potato fries or in sweet potatoes. Put some in Spanish rice, chili, with oranges and other fruits.

Coriander tea is great for digestive problems including upset stomach and gas. It also is good for urinary tract infections. Tea will help headaches and a cold or flu. The seeds promote good sleep so some tea at night would be a great idea if you have insomnia. Coriander is a good source of fiber and it may increase bowel movements. It also helps liver function and stimulates insulin productions lowering blood sugar. Coriander is considered and anti-inflammatory, antiseptic and has high Iron content.

Ginger

Ginger grows as a rhizome underground with lush green leaves above ground. The green leaves don't really matter because it is the rhizome that is used. Most people have seen ginger in the store, it looks like shriveled fingers in light tan and when the skin is peeled off, there is a light smooth texture inside that is usually grated. If the rhizome is too shriveled and hard, it is not good. Go for the plump large "fingers" of ginger and keep them unpeeled in the vegetable drawer for about 3 to 5 weeks. Ginger can also be frozen unpeeled and put in a freezer bag for 6 months. I'm sure most people have seen ground ginger in an airtight container that will last 1 year and candied ginger is sugared and like dried fruit that lasts a few months in an airtight container. I use the candied ginger in my apple pie and it gives it a very lovely flavor. The flavor of ground and grated ginger is warm, sweet and spicy with a little bit of pepper thrown in. It can turn bitter if burned but normally it mellows in cooking.

Ginger is native to Asia and there is a reference to it in ancient Sanskrit. It is greatly used in India, China, the Middle East and it used to be a prized spice in the Roman Empire.

I love ginger tea and make it by stepping 2 ½ slices of peeled ginger in hot water for about 5 minutes. Use fresh ginger in stir fries, in marinades, in fruit salads, and in beverages like iced tea and lemonade. Use it in dipping sauces, in sweet potatoes and squash or add to roasted carrots. Ginger makes a good addition to salad dressings but it is good in desserts like gingerbread, cookies, puddings and cakes.

Ginger is an anti-inflammatory and contains gingerols that give it the nice flavor and lower inflammation responses. It is good for pain and may help those that have arthritis by making them more mobile. Studies are being conducted to see if it can inhibit ovarian cancer cells. Ginger tea helps sinuses during a cold and flu and any infections. Ginger is great for nausea, motion sickness and morning sickness, but should be taken in moderation. Either drink tea or munch on a tiny bit of candied ginger.

Licorice

Licorice is a strong flavor. It is somewhat sweet, tart and a bit like anise and fennel mixed together. I will admit, it is not one of my favorite flavors as I prefer the milder taste of anise, but there are many that absolutely love licorice. Licorice is most known for candy and other sweets but is also put in savory dishes. True licorice comes with a caution and that is licorice poisoning. Licorice contains glycyrrhizin acid or GZA that can cause sickness.

Licorice is also known as sweet root, black beauty, liquorice and 'good old black'. It is a perennial best grown in subtropical or tropical climates. It takes two years to be able to harvest the roots and it may not come back in an area that gets snow. The plants are pretty with oval light green leaves about 3 to 6 inches long that grow opposite on a branch and pretty, purple to blue flowers that produce pods. The part that is used ins the root that looks very woody. It is dried and ground into powder, or you can get it whole and grind it yourself. That black shiny stuff called licorice is not what you want to use because it is processed. Both powder and root, once dried, needs to be stored in an airtight container out of sunlight and away from heat. Another way to get licorice is in an extract.

Licorice has been known as a sweet for thousands of years. It is an integral ingredient in 5 spice powder used in Chinese cooking. In England it was mixed with granulated sugar or other sweeteners and baked into cakes, in Europe the root is chewed as a sweet, in the Middle East and Egypt licorice is used as a drink and it was also used as a medication all the way back to Egyptian times.

The history of licorice used in foods goes way back and it was used to make tea, candy, syrups, sauces and put in custards. It is in cheese and put in fruit dishes as a syrup. It goes well with grilled meats, pot roasts, lamb and wild game and salmon. It is good in baked or mashed sweet potatoes and is even flavorful with chocolate.

Licorice contains GZA, an acid that is absorbed by the body and metabolized through the intestines by bacteria. It can give you a stomachache if you consume too much, so even if you love licorice, keep it down to about once a week in use. This said, pregnant women should avoid licorice. Conversely, a little licorice can soothe an upset stomach and ease problems with food poisoning. It may help heartburn too. It speeds up digestion and is an anti-inflammatory. Something found in a health food store is DGL licorice and it does not have the GZA. This type can be used without problems. Cough drops can be made from licorice and they work well, just watch how many you use. Kids are especially susceptible to true licorice and consumption needs to be limited. Tea should be limited to no more than 8 ounces per day to be safe.

Mace

The spice mace is not the same as the stuff people call pepper spray or mace used to protect themselves. Nor is made from corn, called mace by the Native Americans. The spice mace is part of nutmeg. The nutmeg kernel is inside a shell and covering that shell is a lacy red coating. The red part is peeled off the nutmeg seed, flattened and dried in the sun for about five days to two weeks. The color changes from red to orange amber and is kept whole or ground. That is mace.

The flavor of mace is somewhat like nutmeg but much more delicate and milder yet pungent. It can become bitter if cooked too long. Mace is found ground or in the natural flattened shape called blades that you can grind. Blades keep their flavor longer and it is suggested you only purchase as much as you can use in a six month period of time. It is very hard to grow mace unless you live in a tropical area.

Mace is usually used in sweet dishes and anything that has nutmeg in it can be substituted for mace. It is delicious in cookies and cakes or with fruit and in pie. It is especially delightful when added to puddings and custards. Mace is not just for sweet dishes and can put some real flavor in stews, soups, meats, ceviche, sauces and pickles. It is good with fish, chicken pork, dairy and all types of root vegetables. It is a popular spice in India cuisine.

Mace is an antioxidant and it helps keep the liver healthy. It is helpful with digestive issues including constipation, gas, bloating, nausea and diarrhea. Mace encourages a sluggish appetite and helps circulation of blood in the body. It gets rid of bad breath, is good for the skin and alleviates stress. It helps temporarily stop the pain of a toothache and protects kidneys from stones. It is good in s syrup to stop coughs and is said to help with asthma and arthritis.

Nutmeg

The nutmeg tree is an evergreen tree or shrub native to Indonesia. It was introduced to Europe and was said to be a cure for the plague. The seed is in the shape of an egg about the size of a walnut and the kernel is covered in lacey red coating called mace. Inside is the kernel called nutmeg. It takes about 7 years for a tree/shrub to actually produce the seed or pod, which is sold whole or ground to sell. The seed is better because flavor lasts longer when you grate it yourself. When first harvested, a hole is poked into the seed to remove the oil, which is also sold.

Nutmeg has a warm spicy flavor that is a bit nutty. It is pungent and sweeter than mace. If possible, it is better to add at the end of a recipe that is being cooked so the flavor is better. When baking, this isn't possible, but the flavor is very strong and makes a statement in the food. Nutmeg pares very well with pumpkin and is one of the ingredients in pumpkin pie. It can also be added to pumpkin bread. The spice combines well with cinnamon, cloves and cardamom and is often included in Holiday recipes. It is delicious with stewed fruits or with baked apples or in French toast, muffins and mulled cider. Add to bechamel sauce, eggnog and punch. It goes well with meats, cabbage, potatoes, sweep potatoes, Brussels sprouts, carrots, cauliflower and more.

The oils in nutmeg have anti-inflammatory properties and help joint and muscle pain. Nutmeg is said to calm the body and mine and a pinch in some warm milk or in tea will help insomniacs. Put a pinch in baked beans and other gassy foods to stop flatulence and bloating. It is said to help with depression and stress and is a sedative to lower blood pressure. Nutmeg also gets rid of bad breath and the tea is delicious.

Star Anise

Star Anise not only tastes great it is also pretty to look at. The seed is in the shape of a delicate eight pointed star once it is dried and the whole thing, seed and pods are ground to make the spice. Star anise comes from an evergreen shrub native to China. The fruit is the starshaped pods with a single shiny seed inside. It is found in both the ground form and whole star shape form and has the flavor of mild licorice and anise. Star anise is one of the 5 spices in Chinese 5 spice powder and is very pungent and aromatic. Pods are harvested while green and dried in the sun. Throughout the ages star anise is used in cooking and in medications. In Japan, the bark of the tree is burned as incense.

Star anise is most like to be used in savory dishes with meats and in soups, stews and broths. It is an ingredient in mulled wine. The spice goes very well with tomatoes and fatty meats like pork goose and duck but also is delicious with chicken and eggs. Add to a tropical fruit salad or put some in gingerbread or pumpkin pie for a punch of flavor. Star anise also goes well with root vegetables. The tea is delicious cold or hot. Add near the end of cooking to reserve the flavor and if using the whole star, remove before serving.

Star anise is high in vitamin A and C and is an antioxidant. It is said to fight off a cough or flu and does much to fight aging. It improves digestion, aids in relieving nausea and helps with bloating, gas and constipation by drinking a tea after dinner. It is an anti-inflammatory and one of its components is an antiviral used in the drug Tamiflu to treat influenza. It is also antibacterial and used to fight urinary tract infections, respiratory infections and E. coli.

Conclusion

I hope you have enjoyed the wide variety of incredible Herbs and spices in this book. Be sure to experiment with them and come up with your own favorite uses for them. You now have the power to make sure that your meals are never boring again! Have fun exploring all the different flavors from around the world and make your meals fun and exciting for those you love.

I encourage you to find and use all of the herbs in this book and open your heart, mind and taste buds to new and different flavors. Find the ones that you like the best and use them regularly and often. The best thing about using herbs and spices is that they can enhance your health right along with adding delicious flavors to your meals. Have fun creating.

If you would like professional recipes that use each of the herbs and spices in this book, then be sure to check out my companion book to this one titled: Cooking with Spices and Herbs: 100 Savory Cookbook Recipes Featuring the Best Spices and Herbs from Around the World.

Thanks for reading.

If this book has helped you or someone you know, then I invite you to leave a nice review right now. ***It would be greatly appreciated!***

My Other Books

For more great books simply visit my author page or type my name into the Kindle Store search bar or the Books search bar: **Susan Hollister**

Author Page

USA: https://www.amazon.com/author/susanhollister

UK: http://amzn.to/2qiEzA9

Thanks and Enjoy!

Printed in Poland
by Amazon Fulfillment
Poland Sp. z o.o., Wrocław

53961321R00105